Effective
IEPs
through

WITHDRAWN

CIRCLE TIME

Books are to
the last

*Practical solutions
to writing Individual
Education Plans for
children with emotional
and behavioural
difficulties*

M A R G A R E T
G O L D T H O R P E

F O R E W O R D
J E N N Y M O S L E Y

Effective IEPs through Circle Time
LL 01097
ISBN 1 85503 258 9
© Margaret Goldthorpe
All rights reserved
First published 1998, Reprinted 1999, 2001

Printed in the UK for LDA
LDA, Duke Street, Wisbech, Cambs, PE13 2AE UK
3195 Wilson Drive, NW, Grand Rapids, MI 49544, USA

Contents

Foreword

I am truly delighted to have this opportunity to introduce to you the Quality Circle Time Model and Margaret's work within it. After having been a long serving class teacher, I have spent the last 12 years developing the model to meet the needs of schools to implement a system that could promote self-esteem, self discipline and a true responsibility towards others.

It involves a commitment from schools to the setting up of an ongoing timetabled process of Circle Meetings for adults and children through which to address the key interpersonal and organisational issues affecting a school's development. The model incorporates a range of firm practical strategies and structures to ensure that not only does everyone feel safe and supported, but that they are also offered the chance to take on an equal responsibility for the creation of a positive and caring school ethos. If carefully adhered to, the model has the potential to help everyone feel valued and listened to and to release 'excellence' in all its diverse forms. Over the past decade demand for this approach has grown enormously and with wonderful support from the Calouse Gulbenkian Foundation I was able to train more people to become specialist consultants and trainers in this model.

Margaret's experience as a member of Buckinghamshire's Peripatetic Support Service and Harrow's Behaviour Support Service ensured that she brought to the model a rich range of talents, skills and insights. She immediately understood its potential to meet the challenges of working with the emotional and behavioural needs of certain children 'beyond' the normal range of motivational structures built into this model. Over a period of time she explored, adapted and added a range of ideas so that the weekly class Circle Time meeting could further act as a framework for helping troubled children. Margaret now works with me as an Associate Partner.

'It's a long road to good self-esteem for some children' writes Margaret Goldthorpe. She then goes on to show how, beginning with a single step, this journey is possible. Margaret herself has taken the brilliant step of linking IEPs to the Golden Rules – that is, the school's moral values which help to both simplify and focus the aims and targets for that child. Her proactive strategies are clearly detailed in many practical and useable ideas which special needs co-ordinators and classroom teachers will find invaluable.

Using the Circle Time structures as a forum from which to provide advice and support for a child with emotional and behavioural difficulties is incredibly helpful in removing the burden of implementing IEPs solely from the class teacher. Rather, the whole class become 'partners' in the process of helping one of their team towards his or her aims and targets. Such a positive approach allows the child to experience the pleasure of shared success, to know and enjoy this feeling and to want to experience it again.

My experience of developing Circle Time in schools has revealed time and time again the effectiveness of creating team spirit and a valuing ethos in raising self-esteem. This is an area that is often particularly important for children with special needs, who may have a long history of failure and isolation. It is greatly empowering for children to realise that they have, within themselves and with the support of their peers, the capacity to effect change.

Margaret Goldthorpe's inspiring book will change the task of writing IEPs from being a time consuming necessity to a communal effort that creates a document of real hope that a child's behaviour or learning potential can be changed. I believe that after reading this book teachers and special needs co-ordinators will see IEPs in a far more positive and rewarding light.

Jenny Mosley

This book is one of the projects which evolved from a training initiative set up to support the promotion of the Whole School Circle Time Model. We are very grateful for the financial assistance we received from the Calouste Gulbenkian Foundation. It enabled all of us to talk, study, research, train and be creative!

Acknowledgements

I should like to thank all of the teachers, headteachers and E.P.s with whom I have worked over the last few years in Harrow, in particular: Roxbourne First School; Welldon Park Middle School; Earlsmead First and Middle School; Newton Farm First and Middle School; St. John Fisher R.C. School; Marlborough First and Middle School and Grange Middle School.

I should also like to personally thank: Dennis Goldthorpe, Lucy Nutt and Dawn Price from Alexandra Special School, Harrow; Adrien Abbott, Chris MacDermott and Gill Watts from Roxeth Manor Middle School, Harrow; Nye Toms, Caroline Cordwell, Pat Jones and Elaine Aldridge from Norbury First and Middle School, Harrow; Lys Kirby, Les Olive, Paul Casey, Joanne Healey, Joan Mellor and Donna Bennett from the Behaviour Support Service in Harrow; Jo Browning Wroe and Liam McKay from LDA; and my friend Nicky Wilson.

And of course Jenny Mosley who unfailingly helps, encourages and, best of all **believes** in her staff.

But most of all I should like to thank Dennis my husband and Katie, Sophie, Lotte and Tom, my children, who have helped me so much, and even gave up their whole summer holidays so Mummy could carry on with this book – and who never complained! **Thank you!**

Preface

Of all the difficult jobs that class teachers and SENCOs have to do, one of the most difficult is writing Individual Education Plans for children whose special educational needs include emotional and behavioural difficulties. Whilst we can often think of good aims and targets for them, there are times when we are desperate for good strategies.

There will be few IEPs which concentrate solely on a child's behavioural difficulties; these kinds of problem go hand in hand with learning difficulties. Finding reading and writing hard may well be the first major problem a child meets, and it is indeed a big problem, but they are bound to meet others – we all do. So it is vital to equip the child to meet any difficulties in a way that is not aggressive, does not disrupt others and is not verbally or physically abusive. Otherwise they will have many miserable times ahead of them in adolescence and adult life.

That is why I believe an IEP must not only address any learning difficulties, but also have plenty of strategies to help a child to deal with those difficulties in an acceptable manner both now and throughout their lives.

This practical handbook has been written for all teachers who work in schools using Circle Time and who have to write IEPs for children with behavioural problems. One of the reasons I wanted to write this book was because I had found, whilst working as part of a Behaviour Support Service, that writing IEPs in schools that use in particular the Jenny Mosley Circle Time Model was far more effective than in those that did not. There seems to be an excellent 'fit' between using her Circle Time Model and the devising and implementing of IEPs.

If you have not met the Jenny Mosley Circle Time Model before, it is outlined in Chapter 1. Ideally the model needs to be wholeheartedly adopted by all members of the school community, but for those teachers who want to use the approach and do not have the support of colleagues, a lot can be done within the context of the classroom. To help you obtain more information, other helpful publications and resources are listed in the Resources section at the back of this book (see pp. 104).

I have also addressed this book to newly qualified teachers and those who are still training. Children with challenging behaviour can present a considerable problem to a new teacher and whilst raw energy will carry you some of the way towards addressing difficulties, a thoughtful system may carry you further and, what is more, will last longer than raw energy.

With all of you in mind, I have included as much practical help and advice as possible, to enable you to write and implement genuinely effective IEPs for your pupils who are experiencing significant difficulties with their behaviour.

Introduction

It is 8.20 a.m. one Thursday morning. It is early autumn and it looks as if it might be a beautiful day.

So far things have gone very well. The post brought the news that your electricity bill is being reduced by £10 a month. None of your children announced at 10 to 8 that they needed a Florence Nightingale costume, or the ingredients for a rich fruit cake within the next ten minutes. Even the car was helpful this morning and wasn't making its usual ominous creaking sound every time you turned left.

It's 8.20 on a Thursday morning, you are walking down a sunlit corridor in school and all is right with the world …

… and then Daley walks round the corner, says a cheery, 'Hello, Miss,' and in an instant the whole day is ruined.

It's not Daley's number 1 cut or his forbidden trainers that has ruined your day, it's the sudden reminder that:

- ❍ you haven't written his new IEP, because …
- ❍ at the end of last term you had a review and it was decided that things were getting worse, not better …
- ❍ so, it was decided, because everyone was exhausted, to do something temporary and see how he got on with his new teacher, but …
- ❍ Daley has been outside the head's office at least once a day for the last two weeks and he was on the boys' loos' roof again yesterday …

- so you know he will have to go to stage 4 ...
- that means hours and hours of getting the paperwork up to date, completing the forms and cajoling his teachers, parents and support teacher to come to a review with the EP (educational psychologist), who is more difficult to book than Oasis ...
- everyone is going to want to know what you can suggest to sort out his awful classroom behaviour and stop him from going back on the boys' loos' roof – now!

What makes it worse is that Daley is not the only one. What seems like torrents of children are flowing through the school along the turbulent river of the special needs register. Sometimes it feels as if you are responsible for all of them, on your own.

You are not. You cannot be solely responsible for sorting out all these problems. Neither can you be responsible for coming up with all the good ideas and strategies, and implementing and reviewing them on your own. Not only is it too much for one person, but also there are a lot of people in a school, pupils as well as adults, who have useful skills and good ideas and who need to know it is their responsibility to share them, to help you and Daley.

In order to share responsibility a school needs an ethos which ensures that everyone is listened to and valued. In order to ensure that this happens every day and in all aspects of school life, a school needs not only a vision, but a system.

This system is the essence of Jenny Mosley's Circle Time Model.

1 The model

So what is this system that is going to change your whole school (provided you use it properly) and help you write your IEPs? In this chapter I shall briefly review its structure. The model is described in detail in *Turn Your School Round* by Jenny Mosley, available from LDA.

The application of the model in relation to the children who are experiencing problems with their behaviour, and consequently their learning, will be further discussed as we move along, chapter by chapter.

Circle Time

Circle Time is at the heart of this model. Not everyone will know exactly what it is.

Let us look briefly at what it *isn't*. It isn't carpet time. It is not a time when the children sit cosily on the floor, often with the teacher in a reasonably comfortable chair, and everyone chats about their news or what they are going to do today.

There is absolutely nothing wrong with carpet time – but it isn't Circle Time.

Neither is it a time when the children all talk about their problems, fears and worries, in front of each other, in an **unstructured** way. That would quite naturally terrify any sane teacher.

Circle Time is a listening time. It is not just children listening to a teacher, or quiet children listening to noisy or dominant children; it is a time when each person in the circle has time to speak and space to be quietly listened to in return.

It takes place at a set, **timetabled** time each week. The children and the adults all sit in a circle on chairs of the same height. The whole event follows a set pattern or 'script' and it takes between twenty minutes and half an hour.

If you have never done Circle Time, there is one thing that it is very important to know before you start. Children in primary schools and young people in secondary schools will not be cynical about Circle Time. They deeply value being given the opportunity to share problems and create solutions and they take their role in the implementation of those solutions very seriously.

Do not be cynical – the children and young people do not deserve that from an adult. It cheapens their efforts.

Following the pattern or script is crucial as it enables us to be sure that we are always in control of anything that is said or suggested. It also means the children know where they are in a Circle Time. It promotes the capacity of the circle to Plan, Do and Review.

Structure

So, what is the script?

Opening Game

This will help to pull the group together and provide lots of initial enjoyment. Children will come to love Circle Time and want to use it to tackle their difficulties. One way to encourage this to happen quickly is to make sure things get off to a good start with a lot of **controlled** fun.

Raising the issue during the round

You may already have decided upon the agenda through general school or class planning, e.g., a school-wide initiative against bullying, or you may want to reinforce learning skills. It can help if you have an agenda box in the classroom. Then if you think of something you want to discuss you can jot it down and put it in the box, as can any of the children, although the very little ones would obviously need some help.

This system also provides MDSAs (midday supervisors), other staff, the head-teacher and parents with a place where they can register issues they feel they would like discussed. You have to tell people clearly that not everything is going to get discussed straight away, but at least they can make you aware of what their concerns are.

When you open the Agenda Box at the end of the first week, you will find what looks like the Christmas post and you will probably curse me! However, I can assure you that you will be reminding people to use it by half-term. Be sure that you do.

Once the agenda is settled, each person in the circle has the opportunity to make a contribution to an initial exploration of the issue being considered.

This is achieved by having a conch or **speaking object** to pass round. No one may speak unless they are holding the speaking object.

You can use a soft toy, a small teddy bear, a papier mache or alabaster egg from Oxfam Fair Trade or any object that fits comfortably in the hand and has special significance to the class. Don't assume you know what they will like; I know plenty of year 7 classes that just love soft toys.

At this initial discussion stage it helps to give the group a way of opening the sentence. For example:

> *'I find it easiest to work in class when ...'*
> *'I am happiest at playtime when ...'*
> *'I find it helps me to do my homework if I ...'*

This helps the shyer children get started.

Open Forum

O   After this there is a brief time to discuss the issue freely, maybe five or six minutes.

This part of the Circle Time is known as Open Forum. Make sure the children raise their hands before speaking, listen to each other and speak politely, one at a time.

O   Then comes the problem-solving time.

Each person makes a contribution to solving any problems that have been raised, usually by starting a sentence with one of the following:

> *'Would it help if I ...'*
> *'Would it help if we ...'*
> *'Would it help if you ...'*

The circle can settle upon a plan of action, each person knowing what their role in the action plan is to be.

Celebrate Success

O   There follows a 'thank you' time when anyone in the group may thank anyone else for a kind deed, word or thought they have shown that week. This is also a good time to celebrate success, child to child, adult to child, or child to adult. You may use this time to celebrate any success from last week's targets as well as any other successes the children may have experienced throughout the week.

Ending Ritual

○ The Circle Time usually finishes with another game.

Discipline

Teachers sometimes ask, 'What happens if a child misbehaves during Circle Time?'

The first thing is to remember never to be negative during a Circle Time. I know that sounds a terribly tall order, but it really is important.

For one thing, you are trying to create an atmosphere of trust and sharing. If you are sarcastic, dominant or aggressive the shyer children and those desperate to be good may feel that being quiet or agreeing with Miss or Sir is the best way to avoid displeasure, even in a Circle Time.

The whole point of Circle Time is that it is a time when everybody feels **safe** to say what they feel so that quite brave suggestions may emerge.

This means that everyone is safe from each other's mockery, safe from being interrupted and safe from overt criticism, and also protected against the teacher who is so keen that the Circle Time does not become out of control that they ultimately squash the essential emotional safety and creativity.

This is why the second thing is to remind everyone of the ground rules. These are:

❶ Do not interrupt each other. During the opening round, remember you can speak only if you have the speaking object. That goes for the teacher too.

❷ There is to be no mocking of each other or 'pointy laughter'.

❸ It is central to the model that no child be named in a negative way during a Circle Time. Criticise the behaviour, not the person. For example, Leena may want to say, 'I don't like it when Amy won't let me into her games.' It is better if she says, 'I don't like it when other children won't let me into their games.' This will mean any subsequent discussion on the general theme of sharing games does not have a running undercurrent of hostility between Leena and Amy which may hinder a fruitful discussion.

❹   If a child does not wish to speak they may say 'Pass'. At the end of the round you can say, 'Is there anyone who said pass who would like to speak?'

If there is undesirable behaviour, giggling, slouching or catching each other's eye, the technique of 'adjacent praise' is useful. This means saying to a child who is behaving well and is near the child who is not, something on the following lines:

> *'Well done, I like the way you are sitting up*
> *straight and listening.'*

It may seem hard to believe, but I can promise you the child who is misbehaving will, even if only momentarily, sit up.

At this point, don't waste a nanosecond before looking at the wriggler (or whatever) and saying clearly, 'Well done, now you are sitting up beautifully too. Thank you.'

And smile. Really smile!

I have never known this to fail, even with very difficult year 7 children. The secret is praising the miscreant, however slight the improvement, instantly. They will look surprised, but they will have done what you wanted without being directly confronted, and you won't have spoiled the atmosphere.

This is a case of 'Catch them being good, blink and you'll miss it!'

Another way to deal with inappropriate behaviour is to say:

> *'I can see lots of lovely listening/good eye contact/sitting up*
> *straight … [whatever you want] over on this side of the*
> *circle. Now I can see it here and here. Goodness me, I think*
> *everyone is now listening. Aren't you wonderful!'*

And they will be!

These are only little tricks but they do work and are so much less depressing than bawling, 'Will you shut up and listen!' After that no one feels wonderful – least of all you.

If someone really won't stop being silly, give them a visual warning such as a card with a sad face on it. You can also say:

> *'I am sorry, but if you do that again you*
> *will miss the next game.'*

If they do it again, immediately play a favourite, fast game, excluding them, and then go back to the Circle Time. This also works well.

You will need to teach the children the skills needed for Circle Time – indeed for any learning: the skills of:

- good listening
- good speaking (which includes knowing when not to speak)
- looking skills
- good thinking
- good concentrating.

It helps to run through these skills frequently throughout the week.

Golden Rules

When setting up the Jenny Mosley Circle Time Model in your school it is imperative you establish the Golden Rules first.

We shall look at how the Golden Rules affect your IEP writing in later chapters. Let us first discuss why we have the rules and what they say.

The rules laid out in the model are as follows:

Do be gentle	–	Don't hurt anybody
Do be kind and helpful	–	Don't hurt people's feelings
Do listen	–	Don't interrupt
Do work hard	–	Don't waste your or other people's time
Do look after property	–	Don't waste or damage it
Do be honest	–	Don't cover up the truth

These rules are moral values. They are not the same as safety routines, although those will also have their place. These are 'being' rules as opposed to 'doing' rules.

When a child grows up, we want them to be able to say, 'I am an honest person,' and to know that they are and understand what that means to them. We don't need them to grow up saying, 'I am the sort of person who always walks on the left.' Handy as that is in school, it is not a moral value.

We need to keep the two kinds of rule well apart. It helps to call one kind rules and the other routines.

Be sure you have the Golden Rules put up in every classroom and around the school and playground. (Copies of the Golden Rules for indoor and outdoor use are available from LDA.)

Why are they so helpful?

The main reason is that they mean the whole school can live under the same umbrella of agreed and commonly held values. Anybody, child or adult, in the school can invoke the rules. Everybody, child or adult, knows thcy must abide by the rules.

They are clear and unequivocal. Furthermore, they help children, who must sometimes feel as if the world is full of a million rules.

Children whose behaviour can be challenging may spend some hours each week listening to an assortment of people telling them all the different things they must not do.

> *'Sara, stop fiddling with his pencil case.'*
> *'Sara, stop swinging on your chair chatting to the girls*
> *behind you.'*
> *'Sara, don't keep shouting out and laughing. It means*
> *I have to stop working with other children in order*
> *to tell you off.'*
> *'Sara ...'*
> *'Sara ...'*

And so on and so on.

How much more effective it is to say:

> *'Sara, don't fiddle with your pencil case. We have agreed to*
> *work hard and not waste each other's time.'*
> *'Sara, don't chat to your neighbours. We have agreed to*
> *work hard and not waste each other's time.'*

Not only does Sara hear a consistent message, but the other children also hear a recognised rule being reiterated and therefore reinforced. In addition, if Sara does it again after a warning, and you have to issue a sanction, she will recognise which rule she has broken and what constitutes an infringement.

Instead of the world being filled with a million rules, there are only six, the same six for everyone. Furthermore, you can reinforce good behaviour with the same rules, for instance:

> *'Sara, well done for not chatting, that's really working hard.*
> *Good girl.'*

The secret is to use the words of the Golden Rules both when you have to correct a child and when you praise them.

Incentives

We shall look at incentives more closely in Chapters 4 and 5. It is enough here to say that the incentives are there to reinforce the moral values and make sure that all the adults and children in the school community can praise each other and celebrate each other's achievements.

It is critically important that the words on any stickers or certificates you use are very specific. They must say exactly what it is the child has done that is praiseworthy. For example, if Grace has been trying not to get upset about whom she works with in PE, she could be given a sticker that says, 'We like the way you work with other people.'

This exactness has the added advantage that all adults can now say to Grace, 'Well done, Grace, for working well with others; that is very helpful of you.'

Sanctions

The sanctions system used in this model is straightforward. You make sure all the children in each class have thirty minutes a week of really special time called Golden Time. They will have signed up for an activity to do during this time that they really enjoy. All the activities are specific to Golden Time and are unavailable throughout the rest of the week.

If a child breaks a Golden Rule, they are given a warning, verbal and/or visual. If they do it again, they lose a minute, or maybe two, of their Golden Time.

When it is time for Golden Time, all work is put away. The Golden Time activities are brought out and the children who have lost no time can start playing with the Tomy Train or the Grand Prix game on the computer or whatever they have chosen. The children who have lost time have to sit and look at either a sand-timer or the clock until the time they have lost is past and they too can begin their Golden Time.

This method is simple and it works. You must make sure, however, that the activities are worth having – so no damaged jigsaws from car-boot sales!

You must also ensure that the children have to sit in silence during the time they have lost. This means that you don't tell them off during this time. If you do, it passes the time nicely for them. Watching you get wild again about something they did last Tuesday might well be quite entertaining.

They must know what it feels like to sit still, in silence, doing nothing but looking at a clock for, say, eleven minutes, while their space round the treasured Technic Lego table is just waiting for them. Those minutes will pass very, very slowly.

Next time you can say, 'Emily, stop treading on people's heels in the assembly line. It isn't being gentle. If you do it again you will lose some Golden Time.'

Emily will have to weigh up how much she likes standing on people's heels compared to how much she likes spending twenty minutes drawing on the fancy stationery sheets with the special felt tips – including the glittery pink that always works. If she opts for the short-term pleasure of irritating other people and has to spend nine very slow minutes watching a clock while the fancy stationery table are all writing exotic letters to the Spice Girls, she will have time to reconsider. Next time you ask her not to do something she will have something concrete to weigh this against. She will remember how long those nine minutes were. She will probably decide to lay off Samir's heels.

The great thing about this system is that if you are a good child and don't break the rules, every week you get twenty minutes of really enjoyable Golden Time.

If you want some children to be able to recover some Golden Time they have lost you may want to implement Earning Back Contracts. However, it is important to be aware that for some children with Emotional and Behavioural Difficulties, negotiating their way out of the consequences of their actions is an art they have perfected through years of practice! Also, Earning Back Contracts within the context of an IEP, especially one operated by several teachers may be problematic, as the adults could lose control of the sanctions to the negotiating skill of the child.

Nevertheless, you may consider the child needs to make reparation for something they have done, e.g., bullied another child. In this case the child can make reparations at another agreed time. They may then receive commensurate praise, thanks, acclaim and most importantly forgiveness. However, I believe that for an IEP to work the child needs to know that if they don't want to lose precious minutes of their Golden Time they must heed the warning and not go on to break the rule.

Lunchtimes

Lunchtimes can be a problem. The school day can feel long to children (and staff!), and we ask our children to work hard during all of their lessons. It is therefore important for children to have time and space to play and run about at some time during the day.

Luckily, few teachers now throw all of the children into a barren concrete yard, say, 'Play nicely, children,' and then get cross with the children when what they actually do is either play guerrilla football or cling to the edges of the playground, hoping they won't be struck by a passing ball. In these circumstances playtime is terrifying on a bad day, and on a good day merely dismal.

If you are going to improve your lunchtimes, you may need to have a radical overhaul of the entire system. This means not just painting the playground with colourful patterns, although that is a good start, but thinking about the following:

❶ What do the children actually play in the playground?

❷ What sanctions and reward systems do you have in place for the MDSAs to use?

❸ Are the MDSAs able to access the sanctions and reward systems used by the rest of the staff fully?

❹ Do you have a problem with children thinking the 'dinner ladies' are not as important as the teachers?

❺ Do you have a problem with the MDSAs thinking they are not as important as the teachers?

❻ Do the MDSAs have access to high quality training?

❼ Do you fund this training adequately?

Briefly, the Circle Time Model suggests that MDSAs have their own, paid, Circle Times once each half-term so that they may discuss problems and plan solutions.

It is also important to hold Circle Times with the children on the subject of 'What makes a playtime happy?' It helps to write down all of their suggestions. Have other Circle Times to discuss playtime games. Many children do not know any good playground games. Whereas in the past children could play in the streets and lanes together, that is no longer possible. This means children do not always have an extensive repertoire of group outdoor games.

○ Teachers are encouraged to find and learn some good games to teach the children. The Scout and Guide movement have some good books of games, and parents and grandparents can be asked what they used to play. This works especially well in multicultural schools as the 'fund' of games is even larger.

○ These organised playground games could be taught during PE lessons. This will enable the children to go outside at playtime with a good supply of games they can all play.

○ Some games should be taught to the entire school. This will enable children from different classes and year groups to play together.

○ The MDSAs must also know how to play the games. The instructions for some games could be printed on large cards and laminated. The MDSAs can keep these cards and supply them to the children upon request.

○ The week should be organised so that there are football days and non-football days.

○ On non-football days games such as Danish Long Ball and

basketball should be played. This will encourage the girls to play 'big games'. The rules and skills of these games should be taught in PE.

○ Some days should have no big games. Jacks, ropes, hoops, skittles, air-balls, tennis balls or anything else your children, MDSAs or other staff members think would be enjoyable could be supplied.

○ The playground should be zoned. As well as big games areas, it should have areas for dressing up (even if there are just a few hats and bags); areas where children can sit on rubber-backed carpet squares (it's tiring standing up all the time and not everyone wants to sit in a line on a bench); quiet talking areas; and an area for small games – two-ball, skipping and so on. A good big box of cars to go outside is a useful resource.

○ A cupboard outside for storing toys is useful. MDSAs could help to give out and collect the toys.

○ Playground Patrol should be organised. These are children whom an MDSA can dispatch to hold the hand of a sad child or play with a lonely one. A recruitment drive and training scheme is needed. Older children like this kind of responsibility. This can revolutionise the nature of your playtimes.

○ A community service-type task force should be set up for children who find lunchtimes difficult and who would like to be given jobs and structured tasks.

○ Playground Patrol pupils can be trained in Peer Mediation.

Perhaps the most important thing to remember is this; whenever you have a problem with any aspect of lunchtimes, turn the problem over to the school Circle Times. Ask the teaching staff, the individual class and the MDSAs to discuss problems in their Circle Times.

Sometimes have a Circle Time when representatives of all of these circles come together. Only by addressing problems throughout the school community will you find creative and collectively owned solutions.

When IEPs fail

I have spent some time outlining the Circle Time Model because .thout a behaviour management system in place that you can 'jack-up' for the child who is having difficulties, IEPs can so easily become an exercise in frustration and futility.

IEPs don't work when they are just hoops for a teacher or SENCO to jump through. For example, if you haven't done a stage 2 IEP, you are never going to get any stage 3 help, and what everybody is really after is a statement.

The ones that don't work are the IEPs that are written, signed by everybody and then stuck in the filing cabinet. The next time they are properly looked at is at the review, when it is decided that the child has met none of their targets and needs to go up a stage. What no one is prepared to admit honestly at that point is that they have hardly consulted the IEP since writing it and some of the targets have even been forgotten.

This usually happens because:

❶ The targets were unrealistically optimistic (not TATTs – tiny, achievable, tickable targets).

❷ The strategies were too complicated.

❸ The strategies bore no relation to anything usually done in the classroom and therefore were not at the front of the teacher's mind.

❹ There had never been a real consensus between the teachers concerned as to the nature of the child's difficulties or the appropriate targets and strategies, so no one had ever really owned the IEP. Ultimately all anyone had wanted to do was get the wretched thing written and in the filing cabinet so it could be said to have been done when asking for either stage 3 help or requesting a visit from the EP.

❺ No one had thought to share the whole plan with the child concerned.

❻ No one really expected or wanted the child to hit the targets as it had been tacitly decided that the child is too difficult for the school and needs to go elsewhere.

❼ All the school really wanted was for the child to get a statement because that is the only way to get any extra help, externally funded, in difficult and under-resourced schools.

❽ Lots of children in the class are at different stages of the Code of Practice and no teacher can realistically be expected to keep all of the assorted targets and strategies in mind all of the time.

None of these reasons is unjustified or blameworthy. They just aren't very helpful to the child.

This is why it is important to have a system already in place, and why it is important that you do not put in place something that is going to require you to reinvent your whole classroom practice completely.

What you do with the actual document is also important. I would suggest that first you make three copies. One copy can go in the filing cabinet. You will need quick access to it for reviews, for parents, for when the EP visits and so on.

Give the second copy to the senior MDSA. Make sure they have a ring binder for all of the children's IEPs. There is bound to be something in each one that concerns lunchtime behaviour and the MDSA can't be expected to keep all the lunchtime targets for all of the children in their head at all times. That would be impossible. Also they will need to discuss the targets and strategies with their staff.

If you have been using this model you will have incorporated many of the suggestions for improving lunchtimes into everybody's routines. The MDSAs will not find using stickers or good and bad behaviour notes unusual. It will be what they already do. What happens in the playground will be the same as in the classroom. When you put each IEP into place it will contain the basic strategies you use for all of the children, with a direct focus on the child who needs the extra help.

The third copy of the IEP must go into the classroom with the class teacher. If these targets are to be live and used, then they must be readily to hand.

This is also why they must not be impossibly difficult. When you are extremely busy you don't want to get a document out that is going to overwhelm you with more work and problems. You need to see something that you can do, and within the next ten minutes if necessary.

You need to see a solution, not another problem.

2 Writing the IEP

or

Mark and the lure of overarm bowling

This chapter provides an example of the stages of writing an IEP using a real case history. Before we launch into that, we shall look at the overall structure of an IEP.

Most education authorities have their own IEP forms. Many of these are divided into five sections:

CONCERNS

AIMS

TARGETS

STRATEGIES

REVIEW

If your school is using the whole school Circle Time Model, all of the above categories can be linked together.

First we have our **Concern**. What has caused us to feel this child needs extra attention and care?

It may well be that we are not alone in worrying about this child, other members of staff may have come to us and expressed their concerns. If we are having Staff Circle Times this child's problems may have been raised.

It may well be that problems which relate to this child have surfaced during Circle Time. We may have been discussing playtimes or bullying and, whilst the children will not have mentioned any child by name, the nature of their concerns may have confirmed in us our already existing concerns relating to a particular child.

We may also decide to hold a Circle Time to discuss a particular issue, such as how we work together, playground behaviour, bullying, in order to explore further whether our concerns may also be shared by others in the class.

When we come to construct our IEP it is often difficult to be precise about how we want a child to behave. If we have the Golden Rules we can at this point use them to guide us. Keeping these rules and, even more importantly, knowing how to keep them, and go on keeping them, is our **Aim** for this child. Having a set of clear Golden Rules gives us a clarity of purpose and ambition, both for us and for the child.

When it comes to setting **Targets** for the child the model helps us to address this through suggesting Tiny Achievable Tickable Targets. It gives us practical help with constructing a staged approach to tackling a child's challenging behaviour.

More importantly, however, when we come to construct a **Strategy** which will help us hit our Targets and Achieve our Aims this model gives teachers the chance, through Circle Time, to enlist the help of the entire class, both by using their suggested ideas and their volunteered help and co-operation.

Moreover, the model also suggests many creative and enjoyable Incentives which we can use to both encourage and reward a child's meeting of his Targets.

What is more, the model provides us with a Reward and Sanctions system, through Golden Time, which guides the child with the IEP towards meeting his Targets and achieving his Aims of better keeping, and understanding, the Golden Rules, but will also reward the other children in the class who are not experiencing so many difficulties.

This addresses the understandably unhappy feelings of some children that you don't get any prizes for being good. With this model you get plenty of prizes for being good!

You may also find a Circle Time for children who have special educational needs helpful. There is a chapter relating to this later in the book.

When it is time to **Review** the IEP you can do this through a class Circle Time or through a staff Circle Time.

In order to help plan an IEP using the Jenny Mosley Circle Time Model I have produced the table on the following page.

Planning the IEP

Steps

❶ **Why**	Why are we worried about them?	Concerns	**Circle Time** to discuss child's problem directly or indirectly. Concern may surface during **Circle Time**.
❷ **Where**	Where do we want them to be?	Aims	**Golden Rules** will help you focus on your ambitions for them. You can be idealistic at this point.
❸ **What**	What do we want them to do?	Targets	Select Tiny, Achievable, Tickable Targets. Targets can arise from **Circle Time**.
❹ **How**	How are we going to get them to do this?	Strategies	**Circle Time** will provide many of these. **Incentives** will help you. Use **Golden Time** as a sanction. Have we a strategy for **lunchtimes**? Don't forget **special needs Circle Time**, (see page 86).
❺ **When**	When are we going to see if they are getting there? Date?	Review	Circle Time will help. Maybe have a **staff Circle.**

I think at this point it would help if we had an example to follow through the different stages of writing the IEP. The following is a real case history.

Let us take a look at Mark.

> Mark is in year 6 at a big, city middle school.
>
> He has previously been excluded from two other middle schools. His family have a history of violence and Mark is the victim of violence from both his father and his elder brother.
>
> Mark has just been suspended for three days from his current school for swinging a piece of wood around in the playground. He did not actually hurt anyone but he frightened a number of children.
>
> This is not the first time Mark has misbehaved in the playground. He has sworn, called other people's mothers abusive names, been insolent or rude to the MDSAs and spoiled many children's games. He often pulls his coat up over his head and walks around the playground hiding inside his coat, occasionally swearing at children he passes.
>
> Mark is a pain in the playground and he's not much fun in the classroom either.

We shall now look at how to construct an IEP for Mark.

Concerns

When a child's behaviour is causing concern, either because it is interfering with their learning or with the learning of others in the class, it is usually solely the concern of the class teacher at stage 1 and the class teacher and SENCO at stage 2 to decide on the precise nature of these concerns. By stage 3 there should be some kind of outside agency involved. However, the time such an outside agency (EP or Behaviour Support Teacher) has to offer is maybe so limited as to be almost useless.

So how can we come to an accurate understanding of our concerns?

There are various techniques. You can use fixed interview sampling sheets, frequency count sheets, pupil observation sheets and various types of behaviour profiling sheet. Whilst resource materials are invaluable and readily available from many educational publishers, they often involve only the teachers. When looking at a child's emotional and behavioural difficulties it is probably better to involve all those concerned, that is, the whole class as well as the child.

If you are using the whole school Circle Time Model, at this stage you would hold a Circle Time specifically concentrating on the difficulties that the particular child is experiencing.

It is very important that you ask the child concerned if they mind having a Circle Time to help them with their difficulties. If the child does not want this, you can address the issue in a Circle Time session without personalising it.

In the case of Mark, we asked him at his readmission meeting if he would like to sort out with the rest of his class, during a Circle Time, some of the problems that were plainly making him unhappy. He agreed, saying, 'It's worth a go.'

We also asked the class if they would have a Circle Time for Mark and help him with his problems. They were very keen to do this as his behaviour was causing many of them considerable unhappiness.

At no stage during the following Circle Times did any teacher ever make a negative remark of any sort. The ground rules for Circle Time were adhered to by the adults as well as the pupils. Although Mark was named this was in the context of supportive, helping ideas.

At the beginning of the Circle Time we played some simple circle games.

We then had a round for everyone with the speaking object:

> *'I feel happy in the playground when ...'*

And then a second:

> *'I feel unhappy in the playground when ...'*

A Learning Assistant took notes throughout this time, with the permission of the class.

During the round Mark said that he felt happy when people did not keep leaving him out of things and hating him. He said he felt unhappy when people picked on him. He did not feel able to make a positive comment. He was, however, quite happy to contribute to the circle.

At this point we had a round in which the class was asked to make suggestions to Mark about things that he could do that might help him.

We were aware that this was going to be a time when a great many negative feelings were expressed by Mark's classmates. This proved to be the case. The negative remarks included such things as:

> *'Would it help if you stopped spoiling our games?'*
> *'Would it help if you stopped spitting?'*
> *'Would it help if you stopped pulling at my hood*
> *and ripping it?'*
> *'Would it help if you stopped nicking my crisps out*
> *of my packed lunch?'*

It was important that the children had a chance to express these negative feelings in a safe and controlled place. They were not said in rancour.

There were also other, much more positive suggestions made which we shall come to in a moment. Mark accepted even the negative suggestions with good grace, answering, ''Spose so' to most of them.

We now felt we had a good initial picture of our concerns about Mark, of Mark's concerns and of the concerns the rest of the class had about Mark's behaviour.

In the **Concerns** section in the IEP, we went on to write:

> 1   Mark has few friends and fewer skills in making them.
>   This is making him and the rest of the class unhappy.

We might have been able to write this without a Circle Time, but without the Circle Time these concerns could not honestly have been said to have been discussed and owned by all the class and by Mark himself. Everyone now felt legitimately involved in the process of helping him out of this very unhappy situation.

Aims

By this point it was clear we also now had an **aim**. It was going to be: 'To help Mark feel a sense of belonging in the playground and to find ways of making a friend. We would like him to know how to be kind and gentle, and how good that feeling can be.'

Unlike in target writing, it is possible to be creative and even idealistic at the point of writing an aim, as long as it is directly related to the problem as seen by the child, by the rest of the class and by you. It does not have to be specific; that is the role of the **target**.

It does help, however, if even at this early stage you relate the aim to one of the Golden Rules.

Targets

A great deal has been written about targets. They are at their weakest when they can be described as 'fuzzy', like the following:

> *'She will improve her self-esteem.'*
> *'He will try to manage his behaviour.'*
> *'She will come to understand her own feelings.'*

For a target to be valuable you must be able to see it clearly and know when you have hit it and how near you were to the bull's-eye.

This is not possible with a fuzzy target. Very few of us will ever get to the stage of saying:

> *'Yes, I think I now understand my behaviour.'*
> *'My, but my self-esteem is in cracking good order these days.'*

There are several ways of making sure your target is worthwhile. These are all discussed at some length in Chapter 3.

Before you can test a target, you need to have some targets formulated.

Let us return to our Circle Time (which, by the way, has been running for only a little under fifteen minutes by this time). As well as some of the negative responses, there were plenty of positive ones. This is a small selection from the thirty-two responses from the whole class:

> *'Would it help if you knew you could play with me before playtime started?' (a 'book a friend' idea).*

Mark thought this would help a great deal.

> *'Would it help if you brought your own football and asked us to play during break?'*

His air-ball was permitted by the school and he thought he would like to bring it.

> *'Would it help if Mark didn't always have to go out but could help a teacher inside the school?'*

He liked that idea a great deal.

> *'Would it help if you knew the rules for Danish Long Ball [a favoured game]?'*

There were many more suggestions. Some of these were deeply touching. There were several invitations:

> *'Would it help if you called to play with me after school some evenings?'*
> *'Would you like to help us with the school gardening project?'*
> *'Would it help if I sat next to you in maths?'*

There were several such suggestions, and if they were all carried out Mark, who usually sat alone, would have someone next to him for much more of the school week, and each would be a volunteer, not a conscript.

'Would it help if I taught you overarm bowling?'

This last suggestion was made unexpectedly by the class's best bowler, and made with good grace. At this point Mark just beamed and said, 'Yes, that would be brilliant.'

We asked Mark which of these suggestions he liked the best. He said he liked the idea of knowing whom he was going to be playing with at each lunchtime play. He also said he would like to bring his air-ball in. He would like not to have to go out every lunchtime. And he'd definitely like to learn overarm bowling!

We now felt we were doing very well with the IEP. We had, we felt, some **targets**, and we had some **strategies** built into them.

Holding the speaking object, the class teacher asked if the circle felt that their suggestions for the targets for Mark could be summed up as follows:

❶ Just before he goes outside, Mark will be able to tell his class teacher whom he is going to play with and what he is going to play each Monday, Wednesday and Friday lunchtime.

❷ Keeping the Golden Rules, which are published in the play-ground, Mark will play for fifteen minutes, as agreed. At the end of that time, Mark will present himself to the MDSA, who will give him a smiley face slip of paper if they have no cause for complaint.

❸ During Tuesday lunchtimes Mark will spend fifteen minutes with the gardening group, again observing the Golden Rules at all times.

❹ During Thursday lunchtimes Mark will report to the class teacher, who will discuss with him some indoor tasks they or any other teacher would find helpful.

We asked Mark how he felt about this; he said the summary was fine.

It was made clear to the rest of the group that they had to promise at this stage to carry out all the suggestions they had made in the Circle Time; they were really critically important to the whole plan. They all said they would.

We then played some very unserious Circle Time games and the session finished with a quick round of:

'Is there anyone who would like to thank anyone else for anything they have said during this session?'

Mark thanked everyone, and lots of children thanked Mark, as well as each other and the staff.

ssion took thirty-five minutes. We'd got most of our IEP written and much, much happier.

Strategies

The class teacher and I then spent breaktime, after getting the chairs back round the desks, in writing out the strategies we were going to use to make sure the targets were met.

❶ We had written down what each child had offered to do for Mark. We would make sure he did not fail to have someone to play with each session.

❷ Mark was to have a chart made up that recorded his successes.
   ○ He would get a star for coming, without being asked, to the teacher to say whom he was going to play with before each playtime.
   ○ He would get a star for being able to say what they were going to play.
   ○ He would get two stars if he managed to get the smiley slip from the MDSA.
   ○ When the target-sheet picture was complete, Mark was to be allowed to take it to the headteacher, who would add a headteacher's special award sticker, laminate it and send it home, by post, to Mark's mother, with an accompanying letter of congratulation.

❸ We would have a Circle Time for Mark next week. This would include, 'Last week I said I would … and I managed this by …'.

❹ We decided to initiate at the end of the next Circle Time a secret buddy system to take the heat off Mark. Everyone's name was to go in a hat; each child was to pull a name out of the hat, read it and keep it secret. For the rest of that week they were to do small, secret kind things for their secret buddy.

❺ If Mark infringed the Golden Rules, this would cause him to suffer the same loss of Golden Time that any child would incur.

Our IEP was complete.

Review

The next week's Circle Time revealed that Mark had spent a much better week. He had got eighteen stars and said he felt much happier.

The others in the class had taken their promises very seriously and had even done more than they had promised. One girl said what she had done for Mark was:

> *'I remembered to say "thank you" to him when he held the door open for me.'*

I felt this showed she had a genuinely subtle understanding of how to improve someone's self-esteem.

We introduced the secret buddy system, and agreed to review it at the next week's Circle Time.

We all thanked each other for something done that week.

And so we went on with Mark. Plan, Do, Review. Week after week. Mark planted bulbs in a patch of previously unsavoury beaten earth by the front entrance to the school, he helped the headteacher with piles of filing, he rejuvenated the school fishtank and he nearly mastered overarm bowling.

Most importantly, he found a best friend. It was, surprisingly, a very quiet girl whom he now sits next to every day.

His playground behaviour is much improved and although, like any child, he can occasionally be a little wild, we have been able to return him to stage 1.

Individual Education Plan

No: 1

Pupil's Name: Mark Forbes Class: 6M	N.C. Year: 6
Code of Practice Stage: 1 2③4 5 (Please circle)	Date: 16.10.97

Concerns

1 Mark has few friends and fewer skills for making them.
2 Mark is and the rest of the class are unhappy.
3 Mark bullies other children at playtime.

General aims of provision planned

1 To help Mark feel a sense of belonging in the playground and to find ways of making a friend.

 GOLDEN RULE – DO BE GENTLE.
DON'T HURT ANYBODY.

2 We would like him to know how good feelings of mutual consideration can be.

 GOLDEN RULE – DO BE KIND.
DON'T HURT ANYONE'S FEELINGS.

3 We would like Mark to experience the pleasure of helping things to grow.

 GOLDEN RULE – DO LOOK AFTER THINGS.
DON'T WASTE OR DAMAGE ANYTHING.

Specific targets

1 Just before he goes outside Mark will tell his teacher whom he is going to play with and what he is going to play each Monday, Wednesday and Friday lunchtime.
2 Keeping the Golden Rules, which are published in the playground, Mark will play for 15 minutes as agreed. At the end of 15 minutes Mark will present himself to the MDSA, who will give him a smiley face slip of paper if they have no cause for complaint.
3 During Tuesday lunchtimes Mark will spend 15 minutes with the gardening group, again observing the Golden Rules at all times.

4   During Thursday lunchtimes Mark will report to the class teacher, who will discuss with him some indoor tasks they or any other teacher would find helpful.

Strategies to be used

1   Following the Circle Time we had held for Mark, we wrote down what each child offered to do for Mark. The children are to remember to keep these promises to Mark. (See Chapter 2.)

2   We will make sure he does not fail to have someone to play with each session.

3   Mark will have a chart made up to record his successes.
- He will get a star for telling his teacher whom he is to play with, before each playtime.
- He will get a star for being able to say what they are going to play.
- He will get two stars if he manages to get the smiley slip from the MDSA.
- When the chart is complete, Mark will take it to a teacher, who will add a headteacher's special award sticker, laminate it and send it home, by post, to Mark's mother, with an accompanying letter of congratulation.

4   We will have a Circle Time for Mark next week. This will be 'Last week I said I would ... and I managed this by ...'.

5   At the end of the next Circle Time we will initiate a secret buddy system. Everyone's name will go in a hat; each child will pull a name out of the hat, read it and keep it secret. For the rest of that week they will do small, secret, kind things for their secret buddy.

6   If Mark infringes the Golden Rules this will cause him to suffer the same loss of Golden Time that any child would incur.

Review

Review next week through Circle Time with class. Possible staff review beginning of December 97, i.e. in 2 months' time.

3 Aims and targets

Target setting can be an absolute minefield. It is so difficult when staring at a child's enormous mountain of problems to know where to start. If you are setting targets for a child who behaves beautifully but is not reading as well as they should, your problems can seem less daunting. You are going to make a staged plan that will move the child along the road to becoming a reader. There are lots of very good 'off the shelf' plans for doing this.

If the child has problems with their behaviour as well, this can be when you feel your heart sinking.

Where do you start? In which direction do you go? What are you aiming for exactly, other than just 'Lee will be good'? What do you tackle first?

Let us start at the beginning.

Choosing an aim

How can we consistently choose relevant aims?

Let us look at this systematically. If you are using the model, you will have in place the Golden Rules. These are your school's moral values.

Our overall ambition is for the child to have a clear understanding and acceptance of these moral values.

When a child's behaviour compromises their own or other children's learning or happiness, they will be infringing one of these rules. We need to isolate which of the rules is being infringed. That is not so we can apportion blame, but so we know where we are to direct our help.

Our aim must be to ensure that the child keeps the Golden Rules. What is more, they must understand the rule and what it means to keep it. That is to say, it is not to be a reactive keeping of the rule but a conscious and proactive keeping of the rule.

They must feel that not only do they understand the rules, but also that they know how to keep them. Moreover, they need to feel that they like keeping the rules and know how to go on keeping them.

Therefore when writing the IEP, the aim must directly address the Golden Rule or Rules being infringed. When first using this system, you can do this explicitly. Once everyone is doing it as part of your policy and practice, it can be more implicit.

Keeping our aim and the relevant Golden Rule firmly in mind, we can choose some relevant targets. The targets will help us move the child steadily along the road towards the Golden Rules.

We can't just be at the end of our journey – we need to get there in stages, but the stages must be going in the right direction.

Designing the targets

One of the main reasons for that feeling of 'heartsink' is simply that you have such an enormous job ahead of you. You have many difficulties, both with the child's learning needs and with their behaviour difficulties, and you know that you have to address and even resolve this whole, huge problem.

But you also know that you have to have SMART (specific, measurable, achievable, relevant, time-related) targets or TATTs (tiny, achievable, tickable targets) and they tend to be really tiny steps. So how do you make a small target relevant to a big problem?

Sometimes you find you are addressing the behavioural needs of a girl who swears at the staff, calls out rudely in class, cuts up children's clothes in the cloakroom, barges wildly around the corridors at playtime and won't be called back, with a target that says:

> *'Lizzie will answer politely when her name is called*
> *in registration – on Tuesdays.'*

'Wow,' you think, 'that's really going to make all the difference!'

This target would be all right if you were going to review it every two weeks, but you aren't, you can't. If you were having meetings about all of the children with IEPs every two weeks you'd never have time to take the register, let alone have Lizzie answer to it politely.

I think the first thing to do is make sure your targets are **incremental**. This will ensure they have a bit of shelf life in them.

For example, we may feel Lizzie's targets should be:

① Lizzie will listen to others and not interrupt them.

 GOLDEN RULE – DO LISTEN.
DON'T INTERRUPT.

② Lizzie will not speak rudely or abusively to other people; she will be kind and not hurt people's feelings in this way.

 GOLDEN RULE – DO BE KIND AND HELPFUL.
DON'T HURT PEOPLE'S FEELINGS.

③ Lizzie will treat other people's possessions with respect and not damage them in any way.

 GOLDEN RULE – DO LOOK AFTER PROPERTY.
DON'T WASTE OR DAMAGE IT.

We may then have a Circle Time to help us find some targets.

During the Circle Time Lizzie may say that she feels angry because no one likes her and some people are deliberately cold and unfriendly towards her. She gets rid of this anger by 'hurting' their clothes in the cloakroom. She may also say that she thinks all teachers hate her and she just wants to shout at them.

During the 'Would it help if …' part of the Circle Time, someone may have said 'Would it help if I play a game with you sometimes?' This is an idea which Lizzie may have liked. Someone else may have said, 'Would it help if I asked you to water the plants on the top corridor with me? My day is Tuesday.' Lizzie may have liked that idea too. Her teacher may have said, 'Would it help if I smiled at you as I asked you to answer your name in the register?' Lizzie may well have liked that idea.

Then the initial targets might be:

❶ Lizzie will listen to the person taking the register and she will answer to her name politely and not aggressively. She will do this initially for two mornings a week, rising to each morning and afternoon by the end of eight weeks.

❷ Lizzie will play an interactive maths game with a partner each morning. She will play for five minutes, rising incrementally to ten minutes. She will not shout or swear at her partner during this game.

❸ Lizzie agreed, during Circle Time, to join the team of children who water the plants in the top corridor. She is to water the plants with Gary each Tuesday morning. She is also to take off any dead leaves and tidy up the compost.

These are incremental targets. They give the class teacher a degree of flexibility in helping Lizzie along the road and they also give her targets, and therefore an IEP, with a reasonable shelf-life. The targets are still SMART and TATTs, and they directly address the aim. They are therefore reinforcing two of the targeted Golden Rules. But they are designed to last for eight weeks.

You can't do this with all of your targets, but I would try to make as many of them incremental as possible.

When designing a target, why must it be a TATT?

Targets must be **tiny** or have tiny incremental steps. If the target is not really small or not in really small steps, the child won't be able to manage it. They will get disheartened, you will get cross and feel a failure, and the whole enterprise will end in acrimony.

The target must also be **achievable**. It must be what Vygotsky called in the Zone of Proximal Development. In other words, there is no point in setting a target for a child, even a small target, if it does not start from where the child is.

To put this another way, don't try to make the child run before they can walk, not even just two small steps on a Thursday!

Make sure the target is one you can see and record. It must be something that is both specific and measurable; in other words, it has to be **tickable**.

You now have tiny achievable tickable targets, or TATTs. This gives you a useful strategy.

Because your aim is closely linked to the Golden Rules, every time Lizzie does anything that can be said to be keeping these rules, you can praise her using the words of the Golden Rules. Every time Lizzie speaks to you politely, you can say, 'Well done, Lizzie, for speaking politely. That's really **kind and helpful**.'

This means Lizzie has many more ways of meeting her aim than just the ways you have set out in her targets in her IEP.

However, you have to be constantly watching for ways to do this. Lizzie may have said only three words all week that could reasonably be said to be polite!

You have to be ready to notice and praise anything that is one small step in the right direction.

Catch her being good, blink and you'll miss it!

Ways of choosing a target

Choosing the target, once you have decided which Golden Rule you feel the child infringes most often or most annoyingly, is not an exact science. In the example above one target we chose was fixing the way Lizzie speaks to you at registration. Other teachers on other days may have chosen to fix the way she speaks when asked a question.

What matters is that once you have chosen a target you have made a start along a well-supported route.

To summarise:

1. Look at the Golden Rules to decide which ones the child is breaking most frequently.
2. Decide how they are breaking the rules; in this case one of the ways in which Lizzie is breaking the rules is by not being kind. She is speaking rudely to people, which hurts their feelings.
3. Write aims which will reinforce the Golden Rules you have targeted and directly address the way she manages to break the rules. For example: Lizzie will not speak rudely or abusively to other people; she will be **kind and helpful and not hurt people's feelings** in this way.
4. Choose a target. Using Circle Time, devise something you would like the child to do that is directly related to the rule they are breaking and therefore to the aim. For example, answer the register politely, not aggressively or loudly.
5. Make sure the target can be monitored by someone and, if that is not you, check that any others involved are happy to be part of the target. For example, the target may involve MDSAs, learning assistants, support teachers or the caretaker.
6. The target set must be **incremental**. Make sure that it can be steadily extended from the time of writing until the time of the next review. Be realistic about when this is going to be.
7. Check that it is a **TATT**.

❽ When you have the Circle Time to help discuss the targets, note down the suggestions made by the children in the 'Would it help if …' section. These will help you form your **strategy**.

❾ Make sure you are using all of the other strategies available to you through the model, as discussed in other chapters.

If you are using the whole model you will, as a staff, be using similar strategies with all of the children, not just Lizzie. This means your targets and strategies will fit into a whole school scheme and will not be small, meaningless steps in no particular direction.

Individual Education Plan   No: 2

Pupil's Name: Lizzie Tan Class: 4M	N.C. Year: 4
Code of Practice Stage: 1 2③4 5 (Please circle)	Date: 6.7.97

Concerns

1 Lizzie shouts at the staff, calls out rudely in class.
2 Lizzie cuts up children's clothes in the cloakroom, barges wildly around the corridors at playtime and won't come back when called.

General aims of provision planned

1 Lizzie will listen to others and not interrupt them.

**GOLDEN RULE – DO LISTEN.
DON'T INTERRUPT.**

2 Lizzie will not speak rudely or abusively to other people; she will be kind and not hurt people's feelings in this way.

**GOLDEN RULE – DO BE KIND AND HELPFUL.
DON'T HURT PEOPLE'S FEELINGS.**

3 Lizzie will treat other people's possessions with respect and not damage them in any way.

**GOLDEN RULE – DO LOOK AFTER PROPERTY.
DON'T WASTE OR DAMAGE IT.**

Specific targets

1 Lizzie will listen to the person taking the register and she will answer to her name politely and not aggressively. She will do this initially for 2 mornings a week rising to each morning and afternoon by the end of 8 weeks.
2 Lizzie will play an interactive maths game with a partner each morning. She will play for 5 minutes, rising incrementally to 10 minutes. She will not shout or swear at her partner during this game.
3 Lizzie agreed, during Circle Time, to join the team of children who water

the plants in the top corridor. She is to water the plants with Gary each Tuesday morning. She is also to take off any dead leaves and tidy up the compost.

Strategies to be used

1   We will have two more Circle Times on the subject of keeping the Golden Rule: Do look after property – Don't waste or damage anything. The opening sentences will be:

>   Week 1 'In school, I would hate it if someone damaged my ...', going on to discuss how we could each take responsibility for caring for each other's possessions, and then take collective responsibility.
>   Week 2 'I think we could make the school look better if we ...'; again, this would lead to discussion about how we could each take responsibility for caring for the school and then take collective responsibility.

2   Lizzie will be allowed to stick a fish on the Undersea poster (a target chart available from LDA) each time she manages to play the maths game without being aggressive towards her partner. Her partner will also be allowed to stick on a sticky fish. When the whole chart is complete Lizzie will have 10 minutes' free choice at the end of a chosen day. She will have a letter of commendation from the headteacher sent by post to her home, and she will have a certificate given to her in assembly.

3   Every time Lizzie is spotted by any member of the school staff (teaching, clerical, ancillary, lunchtime) keeping the Golden Rules, she is to be verbally praised, and if possible given an appropriate sticker – especially during lunchtimes and breaktimes. Catch her being good, blink and you'll miss it.

4   Reinforce Lizzie's keeping of the Golden Rules with verbal praise which uses the words of the appropriate rule. For example, every time Lizzie speaks to you politely, say, 'Well done, Lizzie, for speaking politely. That's really kind and helpful.' When she has helped Gary on Tuesday, say, 'Well done, Lizzie, for watering the plants. You look after them really well.'

Review

In six weeks. Please keep notes during Circle Times for discussion in the review and to provide further strategies and/or targets.

4 Strategies

or

broth for all every day

No matter how good a strategy seems to the person who has dreamed it up, it's no use at all to a child or teacher if it's too complicated or labour intensive.

There are times when an outside agency is called in to suggest a strategy for a child who is at stage 3, 4 or 5. The strategies suggested would be absolutely brilliant if you could send the other thirty-five children home for a fortnight's holiday while you and the child concerned got to grips with a complicated series of recording charts, time-sheets and other Byzantine behaviour management techniques. I know; in the past I've suggested them, wise teachers have binned them!

But of course, if you want to change a situation you are going to have to do something.

The most effective method is to have some good systems and strategies for raising self-esteem through celebrating achievement and personal target setting in the classroom, all the time, as a matter of course.

What you mustn't do is create either strategies that are so difficult to manage, you won't do them, or ones that are merely add-ons, alien to the overall philosophy of your classroom. If the strategy is going to be one that helps a child experiencing difficulties to like themself more, work harder and be more cooperative (for example), then surely this is a strategy that we should be employing with all of the children.

If we don't do this, it would be as if a mother said, 'I feed all of my children on watery gruel unless they get ill, when I give them good broth and fresh bread.'

What is therefore important is to have a **whole system** always in place that recognises and celebrates achievement, enhances self-esteem and promotes learning. This is a tall order, I know, and a hard job – and it's our job!

So how are we going to do this? We have taken the first and most important steps:

❶ We have discovered the Circle Time Model, and we have learned how to put it in place.
❷ We have our Golden Rules up and running.
❸ Circle Time is a feature of our classroom life.
❹ We are using Golden Time.
❺ We have made sure our targets are viable.
❻ We have a good system of incentives in place.

So what am I to do about Wesley, who is still out of his seat half the time, interfering with other children's work, never staying on task for more than twenty seconds together, arguing whenever we ask him to do something, fighting in the playground and who loses every pencil we ever give him?

Let us take the example of Wesley for a minute.

The first thing to do is to look through the model and ask ourselves if we are doing it as well as we might. Can we improve upon the ingredients going into the good broth?

Useful checklists might be as follows:

Circle Time:

◖ Am I doing Circle Time regularly?
◖ Am I asking the class to discuss the most important issues?
◖ Am I listening to their suggestions about how we might solve some of our problems and am I implementing their suggestions?
◖ Am I using Circle Time to review how well our plans are working?
◖ Should I have a special Circle Time for Wesley? If so, I had better ask him if he would like this.
◖ Do I need a few Circle Times on the Golden Rules and how we can best keep them?
◖ Do I need a few Circle Times on learning skills and how we can improve them?

If having some good, appropriate Circle Times with the class is going to provide us with some practical, helpful suggestions, then we must put ourselves out to ensure we do them. We may save ourselves a great deal of further work.

Golden Time:

- Do I take Golden Time away from all the children, promptly?
- Do I take it away in small enough amounts for the children who are, like Wesley, frequent offenders?
- Are the activities worth having? Have I found something Wesley likes more than arguing with me and shouting in the classroom? If I haven't, I'm on to a loser with Wesley and Golden Time. Why don't I ask Wesley what he would like for Golden Time and make sure he gets it?
- Do I always give a warning before taking away his Golden Time?
- Do I always relate the rule he has broken to the unacceptable behaviour?
- Do I make all children who have lost Golden Time sit in complete silence and look at the activity they are missing for the duration of the time lost?

Incentives:

- Do I give enough incentives?
- Do I keep a check on who is getting them?
- Could I talk to other people and use some of their ideas? There is nothing more cheering than finding someone else has had a brilliant idea – and then pinching it!
- I know about 'Catch them being good, blink and you'll miss it.' Am I making sure I never miss it?
- Am I really remembering to smile? Is my smile making it to my face?

If I am having difficulty with any of these things, whom can I go to for some help? Am I worried that asking for help looks like failure?

- If you are not having staff Circle Times, this may be a good time to start.
- It may also be a good time to talk with the whole staff to check that your lunchtimes are as well ordered as they possibly can be.

Before writing an IEP for any child in the class, these are some of the things we need to ask ourselves. We need to be brutally honest in our answers.

If we can say that we really feel that we have got our systems in place and running well, and yet Wesley is still wandering around the room, interfering with other children and their work, not staying on task for twenty seconds together and definitely not learning anything like as much as he should be – then maybe we need to look seriously at making him an IEP.

It will not contain anything very different from the programme followed by the rest of the class. What we are saying is, 'The broth is good, it's just that Wesley needs extra help and encouragement to enable him to eat it.'

So, what strategies will help Wesley?

Creating Wesley's IEP

Concerns

As we have just seen, the teacher sees the problem as:

1. Wesley is out of his seat half the time.
2. He is interfering with other children's work.
3. He never stays on task for more than twenty seconds together.
4. He argues whenever we ask him to do something.
5. He is fighting in the playground.
6. He loses every pencil we ever give him.

Aims

We are not going to be able to tackle all of these problems at once. They would be too much to hold in the front of our minds. So what shall we aim for?

▷ We would like him to know how good it feels to complete a piece of work of his own volition. If he did this and we made him aware of how nice it felt, he might want to repeat the pleasurable feeling of personal success.

 GOLDEN RULE – DO WORK HARD.
DON'T WASTE YOUR OR OTHER PEOPLE'S TIME.

▷ We would like him to be able to play happily in the playground with a small group of friends.

GOLDEN RULE – DO BE GENTLE.
DON'T HURT ANYBODY.

At this point, I would leave arguing with the teacher. If we were to achieve the first two and we saw a boy who was happy at playtime, had a few friends, and was getting lots of praise for getting on with his work, there is a fair chance he would not be angry and arguing – if for no other reason than that, with luck, he would not be getting shouted at quite so often.

But I would put in:

> ▷ We would like him to be organised with his pens and pencils.

    GOLDEN RULE – DO LOOK AFTER PROPERTY.
DON'T WASTE OR DAMAGE ANYTHING.

The reasons why I would put this last one in are as follows:

❶ It is a reasonably easy aim to achieve.

❷ We need to do something quickly that Wesley can get right, so we can start to praise him.

❸ It would be less wearing on our nerves if he were better organised and he were not always wasting hours wandering around the room looking for his pencil or 'borrowing' someone else's and thereby starting endless arguments.

❹ If we are really honest with ourselves, we are pretty fed up with Wesley and he is not doing much for our self-esteem. Starting with something achievable for us is probably a good idea.

❺ Also we can put this problem out to tender through Circle Time and get a bit of help from someone else.

Targets

◐ We would like him to be on task for five minutes during a teacher-chosen lesson. This time will rise incrementally to fifteen minutes within six weeks.

◐ We would like him to be able to manage morning play without getting into any fights.

◐ We would like him to have his pencil to hand, ready for the first lesson. (You could make this an incremental target as well; for example, after two weeks he is to have his pencil to hand for the whole of the chosen lesson.)

The advantage of incremental targets is that they give your IEP a longer life. We are always being told to make the targets small – but that means forever updating the IEP as targets are met. As we know, that is not going to happen. So the IEP will become a redundant and forgotten document – understandably. Incremental targets can help prevent that.

Strategies

To help his playtime behaviour:

- ○ We will have a Circle Time much like the one we had for Mark. If that proves impossible because Wesley does not want it, we will have a general Circle Time on the subject of 'What helps us to have a happy playtime'.
- ○ We will keep in mind the strategies suggested in Mark's Circle Time (see Chapter 2). When it is our turn to speak during the 'Would it help if I ... Would it help if you ...' section, we will suggest some of those strategies.
- ○ All suggestions made by the class will be written down and kept for further reference.
- ○ We will ensure that Wesley has someone to play with before he goes outside for morning play, and knows what he is going to play.
- ○ He is to ask the teacher on duty if he has been well behaved during morning play. If he has, he is to ask them to give him one of their 'good playtime' stickers (no one should go out on duty without a pocketful of these stickers – Wesley will not be the only child whose playtimes can be monitored in this way). When he comes in from play, his teacher will look to see if he has got a sticker and praise him if he has.
- ○ You may want to record this on a target-sheet (you could photocopy one from the book of photocopiable materials available from Jenny Mosley Consultancies, address at the back of the book). On the other hand, you may think that as you are using a target-sheet for his on-task behaviour you can't be doing with any more charts.
- ○ Even if you don't want to use a chart, it is a good idea to have some means of recording his successes. A quick way is

to put a mark next to his name in your mark book, with the date. One of those felt tip stamper pens with smiley faces or stars or whatever is useful for this. Keep a key at the bottom of the page to show what the smiley face means. Using this method, you can have several children using this technique at one time. But don't forget that **praise** is the motivating strategy; the stamp is for your benefit when it comes to any review. So remember to say:

'Well done for playing happily in the playground, you didn't hurt anybody and you were really gentle. Good boy, I'm proud of you.'

And smile, all the way to your eyes!

Remember – what you say and how you say it is every bit as important as what the child does and how you record it.

To increase his on-task time use Listen, Repeat, Return, Complete technique

- First arm yourself with a kitchen timer, preferably the kind that rings. (They cost about £5 in hardware shops, but you'll get years of use out of one.)
- Sit Wesley near, if possible next, to you.
- Tell him the work you want him to do.
- Get him to repeat this back to you *exactly*, (you may have to tell him two or three times, but eventually he must repeat it back to you exactly).
- Turn the ringer to five minutes.
- Tell Wesley he is not to move, just work until the timer rings. (If you forget he is there, the ringer will remind you.)
- When the timer rings, if he is still sitting there doing what you asked him to do give him a big smile and lots of praise, and stamp a smiley face on his chart.

Don't worry about how much work he has done. We are just helping him to learn to sit at the task at this point.

- Tell him every time he gets four smiles he can show it to the headteacher (or six, or whatever you think the head can reasonably stand).

- When he has got three headteacher stamps or stickers, laminate the chart.
- Post his chart to his parents with a letter of congratulation.
- Tell him that the time will be going up by two minutes each week, and by three after six weeks.
- If you have to sit with him, smiling and being encouraging for the first day to ensure he manages to be successful – do it! It will be worth it in the long run.
- Tell the class at every opportunity how well he is doing and always in Circle Time.
- When praising him, always tell him how well he is keeping the three Golden Rules we are targeting.
- This technique works well, provided you keep the ringer out of reach when not in use! (See the photocopiable section at the back of the book for further information on this technique.)

We are now up to the last of our three targets. How are we to get him to remember his pencil?

So far the work you have to do to run this IEP is as follows:

1. Before each morning play ask him whom he is playing with and what they are going to play. Stamp his chart and praise him.
2. Put the ringer on for five minutes each day and keep your eye on him for the required amount of time, stamp a chart and smile.

In my experience that's enough!

Get some help with the pencil problem.

Helping Wesley to be more personally organised using Circle Time

We have already seen through looking at the case of Mark how a Circle Time can help a child who is facing difficulties and how it can help us write a realistic IEP. Mark is a real case and not an isolated one.

When the strategies come from a class or staff or special needs Circle Time, we know we can put them into practice because in these cases targets are being backed up by individuals who are undertaking to do something helpful.

The strategies are suggested by children or, at times, adults, in front of each other and written down. They can be pinned to the classroom wall with names attached to suggestions and offers of help. They are **live** strategies and they are **owned**.

What is more, they are coming as a result of Circle Time and are therefore part of your usual classroom routine.

Teachers cannot take responsibility for doing everything for everyone in a classroom. That applies as much to putting IEPs into practice as it does to washing the paint pots or giving out the maths books. A teacher might have overall responsibility for a child's learning and behaviour but they cannot be expected to do it all alone. We are each here to help each other and Circle Time gives us the opportunity to learn and practise this.

For example, one of Wesley's problems is that he never has a pencil, rubber or ruler ready for work in the morning.

> ❍ During the next Circle Time say clearly, 'Wesley needs help sorting out his pencil case every morning.'
> ❍ Someone will definitely say: 'Would it help if I sorted out your pencil case with you?'

That was our **target**:

> *'Wesley will have all the correct equipment ready for class.'*

It has been accompanied by a viable **strategy**:

> *'Darren will help him look through his pencil case each morning.'*

> ❍ How you rectify any deficiencies found will depend upon school policy; give him a replacement pencil, ask someone to supply one from home through his Link Book, or whatever. At least you will not be in the situation of discovering twenty minutes into the lesson that he has not got a pencil – again. What is more, the situation is being initially addressed by someone other than you.
> ❍ Then, if twenty minutes into the lesson you discover he hasn't got a pencil, you can reasonably remind both Wesley and Darren that they kindly offered to check through Wesley's pencil case each morning. They know this is so

because you wrote it down during Circle Time. If they have remembered you must smile, praise and thank them.

- If they remember to do it for two or three days, it would be easy to give them a 'Thank you for being helpful' sticker each as a reward and to encourage them to keep on doing it, at least until Wesley is more in the habit of having his pencil in his hand at the right time.
- Remembering to give two stickers is a chore but it is less nerve jangling than shouting at Wesley every day about his wretched pencil.
- In addition you have the benefit of Darren seeing himself as a helpful person – and he's got the stickers to prove it!

Strategy writing without Circle Time

If, on the other hand, you had been writing some IEP targets and strategies without the benefit of a Circle Time, they would have read something like this:

Target: Wesley will have his pencils, rubber and ruler with him each day.

Strategy: *Either* I will remind him to have a pencil to hand each morning.

Or I will ask someone to help him find a pencil each morning.

In either case the teacher is having to take the initiative and in the second case you also have the problem of involving a conscript rather than a volunteer. The only person who owns this particular strategy is you.

This is not going to take away the problem of Wesley and the pencil; it is going to give you the problem of policing Wesley's pencil.

This is often the problem with strategies that are teacher dependent. We know we have to be realistic and remember that there are lots of children in the class. It's no good inventing a bunch of tricky strategies that are going to prove impossible to administer. At the same time, we know we have to make sure the child meets the targets we have set and that is going to need a plan of action.

This means that if for some reason we cannot enlist help through a Circle Time, we are going to have to keep any strategy small, 'do-able' and in the front of our minds.

Using praise as a strategy

If we felt we had no one in our class with Darren's splendid organisational skills, we would have to rely on our own skill to get Wesley to have his pencil in his hand when needed.

We know there is no point in dreaming up a complicated teacher-led system for doing this involving any more tick charts; the chances are it will only fail and then we will be in the unhelpful situation of being cross with ourselves – as well as with Wesley.

So we must remember: 'Catch him being good, blink and you'll miss it.'

- In other words, every time you say 'pencil' to Wesley and he has gone and found one, and every time you spot Wesley with a pencil in his hand at the right time, you have to notice it and you have to give him lavish praise and smiles.
- Once or twice a week you also have to remember to slap a sticker on his jumper that says, 'We like the way you have been responsible' and give him a beaming smile. The chances are that if he has been remembering his pencil a bit more often you will actually want to smile at him!
- It would also be helpful to mention how well he is doing during a Circle Time – even if he is only little bit better!
- You could also get Wesley to write on a leaf that he is remembering his pencil these days and put it on a 'I am pleased with myself because ...' tree displayed in the classroom.

In other words, there are ways of changing someone's behaviour that are not always going to involve you in undertaking a complicated strategy that is so teacher intensive it is bound to fail.

One of the problems with altering a child's behaviour is that we are apt to notice everything they do that we don't want them to do and fail to notice and point out everything they do that we **do** want them to do.

The secret is in the noticing; not just you noticing that the child is doing whatever it is you want them to do, but also getting the child to notice that they are doing it and to feel pleased with themself – so pleased they want to do it again; so pleased – because they know ***how*** to do it again.

Pointing it out, through smiles and praise, is the easiest way, but you **have to do it every time**.

If you are going to use praise in this constructive way, you have to remember that:

❶ The praise must always be specific; for example: 'Well done for remembering your pencil, Wesley.'

❷ The praise must always be accompanied by eye contact and a smile.

❸ You need the child to like themself for what they have just done and to like the feeling that gives them enough for them to want to go out of their way to find opportunities to do it again.

❹ And when they do it again you have to praise them in the same way – again.

❺ And again.

❻ And again!

This can be difficult. It can feel a bit Pollyanna-ish to go about noticing the good things all the time and pointing them out and praising them, but it's a lot less depressing than noticing the bad things all the time – which is what we can end up doing.

It is of course true that not having a pencil at the right time is a very minor problem compared with some of the things Wesley regularly gets up to. However, what you are trying to do is to start by finding something that you can put right in order to be able to praise him and help him know how good praise can make him feel. What is more, if you used the first method and Darren is doing his stuff, Wesley will also know how nice it feels when someone wants to put themself out to help you.

Praising using the Golden Rules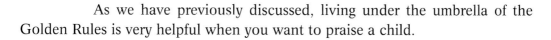

As we have previously discussed, living under the umbrella of the Golden Rules is very helpful when you want to praise a child.

▶ In the case of Wesley, first we catch him sitting ready to start his work with his pencil in his hand.

▶ Then we can say, 'Well done, Wesley, for having your pencil, not wasting time and being ready to work hard. Good boy. Thank you!' And smile.

All of the Golden Rules can be used this way.

▶ First we catch Darren helping Wesley.

- Then we say, 'Thank you for helping Wesley with his pencil. It was very kind of you.'
- This has the benefit of being specific, reinforcing the Golden Rules and raising the child's self-esteem, all in one go.
- If Darren is later unkind to someone, we can say, 'That was an unkind thing for a kind boy like you to have done.'
- And, with luck, Darren will recognise that he is a kind boy, having been told so on so many occasions that he now believes it of himself. If this is the case, he will be able to acknowledge his unkind behaviour, apologise and know he is able to go on being kind.

Individual Education Plan

No: 4

Pupil's Name: Wesley Hamilton Class: 4M   N.C. Year: 4

Code of Practice Stage: 1 2③4 5 (Please circle)   Date: 20.1.98

Concerns

1 Wesley is frequently out of his seat.
2 He interferes with other children's work.
3 He has great difficulty in staying on task.
4 He argues if he does not like the requests made to him.
5 He frequently fights in the playground.
6 He loses every pencil we ever give him.

General aims of provision planned

1 We would like Wesley to know how good it feels to complete a piece of work of his own volition.

 GOLDEN RULES – DO WORK HARD.
DON'T WASTE YOUR OR OTHER PEOPLE'S TIME.

2 We would like him to be able to play happily in the playground with a small group of friends.

 GOLDEN RULE – DO BE GENTLE.
DON'T HURT ANYBODY.

3 We would like him to be organised with his pens and pencils.

 GOLDEN RULE – DO LOOK AFTER PROPERTY.
DON'T WASTE OR DAMAGE ANYTHING.

Specific targets

1 We would like him to be on task for 5 minutes during a teacher-chosen lesson. This time will rise incrementally to 15 minutes within 6 weeks.
2 We would like him to be able to manage 10 minutes of each morning playtime without getting into any fights. This will rise to all the morning

playtime and then go on to include afternoon playtime as the year progresses, subject to consideration at each review.

3   We would like him to have his pencil to hand, ready for the first lesson. After 2 weeks he is to have his pencil to hand for the whole of the chosen lesson.

Strategies to be used

1   We will have a special Circle Time for Wesley. If he does not want that we will have a general Circle Time on the subject of 'What helps us to have a happy playtime.'

2   We will keep in mind the strategies suggested in Mark's Circle Time (See Chapter 2). When it is our turn to speak during the 'Would it help if I ... Would it help if you ...' section, we will suggest some of those strategies.

3   We will ensure Wesley has someone to play with before he goes outside for morning play, and knows what he is going to play.

4   He is to ask the teacher on duty if he has been well behaved during morning play, and if he has, can they please give him a 'good playtime' sticker. When he comes in from play his teacher will look to see if he has got a sticker, praise him if he has, and record it, using a recording chart, (ready made charts are available in Photocopiable Materials for use with the Jenny Mosley Circle Time Model).

5   His teacher is to use the ringer to increase his on-task time. (See instructions for Listen – Repeat – Return – Complete, p100.) Every time he gets 4 smiles, he will show the chart to the headteacher. When he has got 3 headteacher stamps or stickers, the chart will be laminated and posted home to his parents with a letter of congratulation.

6   When praising him we will always tell him how well he is keeping the 3 Golden Rules we are targeting.

7   Darren will help Wesley remember his pencil.

Review

Briefly review after Circle Time on playtimes. Keep notes during Circle Times as these will inform further target setting and strategy planning. All staff concerned to review 3 weeks before end of term.

5 Incentives as strategies

or

no more 'Man overboard!'

On some IEP forms you will see there is a section called 'Motivation strategy'. What this really means is, how are you going to persuade a child to do what you want? In other words, what's going to be in it for them?

This is a really important question and one you must never fail to ask yourself. If we are asking a child to give up behaviour which they have found rewarding in some way in favour of behaviour which only we will find rewarding, it won't happen. The child has to find the new behaviour rewarding too. So we must make sure there are plenty of rewards.

At this point you can start to get led astray by token economies.

- It's a dangerous route, especially if it's your only route.
- If you do go down this road, you are going to risk them only doing what you want when you are around to reward them.
- Or, you will risk them only ever doing what people want them to do when they get a prize given to them.

What you really want is for them to behave in a certain way because:

1. They know it is right.
2. They like themself better and feel really good when they do what is right.
3. They know how to do it again and again wherever they are and like the feeling it gives them every time.

This is a long-haul route. But it's really the only one worth following.

So what kind of motivation are we going to provide?

One of the best ways of consistently motivating children is to surround them constantly with celebration and recognition of their successes in both their work and their behaviour.

However, we must do the same for all children, including those whose behaviour is as we would want. Otherwise it just isn't fair. We cannot afford to let the reward differentials become too great any more than we can let the gap between the behaviour of the 'good' children and those we perceive as 'difficult' widen. We all have to move along with each other.

If we imagine that the years from Reception to 12 are a long journey, we have to ensure that everyone involved, parents as well as children, can make the journey to the end without leaving anyone behind. This means while we are on this journey we have to keep the whole party together.

We have to make sure that all of the children have not only the necessary equipment for the journey, such as good social skills and learning skills, but also good morale. We have to ensure they want to stay with it even through the difficult times.

To do that they must feel valued and wanted. In other words – they must have good self-esteem.

If a child is to stay the course for all those years, they are going to have to feel that they are having a good time and that everyone wants them. This, translated into school terms, means we have to make sure that children and their parents feel wanted and successful.

So how are we to keep children travelling along with us and not dropping by the wayside?

First, we must know where this journey is heading.

- ❍ We are aiming for children to see their own success in terms of being able to live by a set of moral values we call the Golden Rules. If, when children finally leave school, they have internalised these rules and are able to live their lives with a sure understanding of what these rules mean and how to keep them (even if they don't *always* manage it), then we will be able to consider their school life has been successful.

- ❍ This includes academic success – Do work hard. Don't waste your or other people's time – but it is not exclusively academic success that matters. This means that all children can be a success at school because that success is not dependent upon just passing exams or getting good marks.

Secondly, we must know how to stop people feeling left behind or 'not wanted on voyage'.

> ○ If the rules of our journey through school are 'Arrive knowing how to be clean, be quiet and be clever and have parents who can keep up to the demands made on them through the endless letters home (sign this – contribute to that – help with the other)', then it is not going to be long before we have children and parents deciding they are on the wrong boat and getting off at the next opportunity.
> ○ We have Circle Time to help each other over difficulties and help to solve each other's problems. Circle Time is also a place where we can practice social and learning skills.

Thirdly, we must have a way of rewarding those who stick by the rules and a way of checking those who are making the journey hard for themselves or others.

> ○ Golden Time is there both to reward and to discipline children. Golden Time is a **concrete** way of showing children what is otherwise a rather **abstract** notion, that the school community values the effort it takes to keep the Golden Rules – what is more, if you don't make that effort you will lose that privilege. Even if what you do wrong is really quite minor – unkind teasing, for example – it is still going to lose you special time. This helps keep the party together as it travels along. Everyone is being constantly kept up to the mark and the rules apply to all.
> ○ This also means that if you are not so bright and a bit mucky you can still be a star because you can keep the Golden Rules well.

It is often said that children who find reading, for example, difficult and who spend their time dancing about the room, calling out or disrupting the work of others are doing so to avoid doing the work they find hard. I am not at all sure this is the case. There are a great many children who find reading, writing, spelling and so on very difficult indeed but do not in any way disrupt the work of the class.

I think it is more the case that the child who has difficulties but does not disrupt can accept their difficulties because they get good feelings about themself from other sources. They have such a good supply of self-worth that they can say to themselves, 'OK, so I'm not brilliant at reading and writing, but I'm kind, I look after people, I'm reliable and work hard and I'm always truthful. I like myself well enough and I feel I have a valued place in this classroom or family. I can handle finding reading difficult – it's not the end of the world.' They may not articulate this feeling in words but they are demonstrating it through their behaviour.

The child who is dancing around the room, calling out and so on does not feel this way about themself. It is up to us to redress this. We must find many ways to praise them and to make sure all of their achievements are celebrated.

Some ways of celebrating achievement

I have divided this section into four parts:

❶ Ways of celebrating the achievements of the whole class.
❷ Ways of celebrating an individual child's achievement.
❸ Ways for a child to celebrate their own achievement.
❹ And lastly, but most importantly, ways of letting parents know about a child's success. They have to want to stay on the boat too.

Ways for the MDSAs to celebrate children's achievement can be found in Chapter 7, which is devoted to their role in the successful implementation of IEPs.

There are lots of other ideas in the books mentioned in the reading list at the back of this book.

Ways of celebrating the achievements of the whole class

Why are we talking about the achievements of the whole class in relation to writing a child's IEP?

○ One reason is – the more we celebrate everyone's achievement, the fewer IEPs we shall have to write.
○ Secondly, this will mean, as we have said before, that you are not having to remember to do something different; there will be no bizarre add-ons to your usual classroom practice.

If we have some good systems for celebrating achievement already in place, when we write the IEP we can select a few for more intense and focused use.

A praise tree:

Cut out a large tree shape from brown sugar paper. Make sure the trunk and branches fill a whole noticeboard. Cut out some leaf shapes from green paper, make these about 7·5 cm long by 5 cm wide. Then select one thing you feel needs improving in the classroom, for example one of:

- listening
- being kind
- staying in your seat
- lining up quietly
- putting up your hand and not calling out
- remembering to say 'please' and 'thank you'
- not fiddling with each other during a story
- getting back to your places quickly after assembly or playtime
- whatever else you choose.

Then say to the class:

> *'Every time you feel you have [for example] been kind, go and get a leaf, write your name on it and put it on the tree with a drawing pin.'*

You can vary this by having older children write on the leaf the kind action they performed. You can also say that if a child spots someone else (not their best friend) doing something kind, they can put a leaf up for that, with an explanation.

You can add:

> *'If the whole class or a large group in the class manages to be kind [for example, looking after a new child, helping with younger children's assembly or sports day, sorting out a library corner or whatever] then you can have a large flower on the tree.'*

Give them a time limit of perhaps half a term. You will then be able to say:

> *'Let's see how beautiful we can make our praise tree look by then.'*

If the tree is stunning, it may be worth taking a photograph of it and having it made into a poster for permanent display or to travel with the class to their next year – to remind them at all times that they are a kind class.

You may have started this as a strategy for a child who has to have an IEP for being a bully. Whilst it will help them to improve, especially if you remind them to put their leaves up if you see them managing even small acts of kindness, it will also mean that the whole class are focusing together on kindness.

You are giving one child special attention – but only you really know this. They are not being singled out again, but they are having their target especially well supported by a viable strategy.

You can also use these trees as trees of achievement or for reinforcing the keeping of the Golden Rules.

Prepared posters:

You could have other ways of recording successes. For example, LDA produce two Class Target Sheets. One is an undersea poster with reusable sticky fishes. You can use it in the same way as you used the tree; you stick a fish on the undersea picture every time the particular target chosen is met. The other is of the night sky with reusable stick-on stars. The advantage of the LDA reusable pictures is that you can grab one from the stock cupboard and get on with using it as soon as you decide you need it, without having to spend hours cutting out trees, leaves, fishes or stars.

School praise tree:

A tree such as the one described above could be placed in a central position in the school. In this way the whole school could focus on a particular target and gain a sense of collective pride as visitors to the school would be able to see all of the acts of kindness, or whatever has been chosen, being celebrated.

If you wanted to, you could put the use of this central tree onto every IEP currently in operation in the school – whole school strategy.

Golden scroll:

Find a large piece of sugar paper. Make sure it is not in too dark a colour or the writing will not show up. Put the name of a child at the top. If you are doing this as part of a child's IEP do not make that child the first one with whom you use this idea. If you do they will guess it's a put-up job and be unimpressed. Instead, use this idea with two or three other children first and then extend it to the child on the IEP.

Put the scroll on a desk or table at the side of the room. Ask all of the children to write on the scroll. Tell them they are to write something they like about the child whose scroll it is. Provide them with a thick gold marker pen. If you want, you can write the first statement at the top, to demonstrate what you mean.

If you do not trust your class not to write inappropriate remarks while you are not looking, have the scroll out only whilst you are in the class. Otherwise you can leave it out throughout the day.

At the end of the day present the scroll to the child concerned with great ceremony. Tell them this is what their classmates feel about them, and that if they are ever feeling fed up they can get it out and read it. Tell them to keep it safe. Then get the whole class to give them a clap.

I have used this a great deal with considerable success. However, if you have a child with very low self-esteem you may find when you give the scroll to them they rip it up. Do not be surprised by this.

What you must **not** do is:

- Shout at the child.
- Think to yourself, 'I wish I hadn't done that, all I have done is made it worse.'

You have not made things worse.

What you should do is to collect the bits calmly and say very nicely to the child:

> *'I know you have ripped up the scroll, but the others still think those nice things about you. I will mend this and, when you feel you want it, come to me and we'll read it through together again. Then you can take it home. Don't worry.'*

And smile.

The child may well reply by telling you they don't care and they will never want the scroll. If so, tell them kindly that you will keep it for them, safely, in case they should change their mind.

You should do this with any work the child destroys after you have praised it:

> *'I know you have ripped it up, but it was still a good picture [or piece of maths or whatever].'*

It's a long road to good self-esteem for some children. But every journey begins with a single step and some journeys take many years – one step after another. The thing we have to remember is that it's their journey, not ours. Just because it's taking a long time, that does not mean there is anything wrong with our teaching. It's just that they have a long road to travel.

Golden Chair:

During a Circle Time put a chair in the middle of the circle and throw some attractive cloth over it. Now sit a child on the chair and ask the children in the circle to ask questions of the child in the Golden Chair. These will depend on the child's age and may be questions such as:

'What's your favourite food?'
'Who is your favourite Spice Girl?'
'What's the name of your favourite teddy?'

The important thing is that this is another way of helping the child to feel special and important.

Again, do this once or twice with other children before you choose the child you are targeting.

Ways of celebrating an individual child's achievement

Clear and precise stickers:

Stickers can turn a child into a message board for their own success – but only if they are really specific. There is little point in walking about the school with a sticker on your jumper if all it says is 'Wow'. Wow what? It doesn't mean much to the casual passer-by.

If you have a sticker that says, quite clearly, 'Thank you for staying calm', then any adult in the school can say, 'Well done, I'm really pleased you managed to stay calm.' That applies even if they don't know all of the circumstances. If one of your IEP targets is about staying calm under pressure, then everyone who sees a child with a sticker indicating success is going to be able to praise their efforts.

That means the IEP targets for that child are not stuck in the filing cabinet – they are plastered to the child's chest! You don't get more 'live' than that.

There are lots of stickers available from LDA that will reinforce an IEP target or indicate the nature of the targets, as well as others which praise the use of the Golden Rules. The use of these stickers can form part of your strategy to implement the aims and targets of your IEP. When you are writing your IEP, the knowledge that you have these stickers at your disposal can help you phrase the target in such a way that the sticker can act as a reward for meeting the target.

You could use the sticker as a reward for, say, managing to stand in the assembly line calmly for three consecutive days.

You could use the sticker to reward quickly a child who has managed to stand calmly in the assembly line for two minutes – and that's the first time they have managed even that. Maybe you feel they need a quick reward to help them see exactly what is you want them to do. That gives a kind of kick-start.

You may also want to give a sticker to a child who needs no IEP but who you feel is slipping a little. By giving them a sticker which says, 'We like the way you stand in line calmly' you may keep them behaving in the way you prefer and prevent them from joining the attractive gang of ankle-kickers and line-jostlers. You will have praised them publicly for their good behaviour and reminded them of how nice this praise feels. What is more, they will go home with this good news emblazoned on their jumper. Hopefully their mum will give them a big kiss and so further reinforce your efforts.

You may want to reward a child who always stands in line calmly. Just because they always manage to behave well, that doesn't mean they don't deserve a special sticker.

For example, there are stickers that say:

- Well done for working with other people
- Well done for staying calm
- Well done for listening well today
- Well done for being kind
- Well done for being a great class member
- Well done for being honest
- Well done for being helpful
- Well done for good work
- Well done for tidying up
- Well done for caring for your school

There are other stickers that begin, 'We like ...'. These can be given by any adult in the school, either for meeting an IEP target or to reinforce general good behaviour.

If a whole class has been involved in helping to set the IEP targets during a Circle Time, as we saw with Mark, and they have also suggested ways of helping a child meet these targets, then these stickers can be given by the class during a subsequent Circle Time. They will then feel that they are all rewarding the child.

Stickers suitable for this kind of use are:

- We like the way you kept your temper
- We like the way you stand in line calmly
- We like the way you finished more quickly
- We like the way you have been responsible
- We like the way you are a good friend
- We like your table manners
- We like the way you are so helpful
- We like the way you play well

- We like the way you are so polite
- We like the way you look after the playground

These stickers can also be kept in mind when setting targets for IEPs.

Target badges:

There are also pin-on badges available from LDA which indicate a child's intentions for their own behaviour.

After discussing the child's IEP with them, you can consider the targets they have to meet. If they would like, they can then have a pin-on badge to wear for a couple of weeks to show people what they are trying to achieve.

This means if any adult sees them meeting their target, they can instantly praise the child, using the words on the IEP target, because they will be the same as the words on the badge.

These badges say things like:

- I am trying to be kind today
- I am trying to keep the playground rules.
- I am trying to work hard
- I am trying to be calm today

Certificates:

The advantages of issuing certificates are numerous:

- You can give them out in class or in front of the whole school. Provided you do this with due ceremony you will do a great deal to raise a child's self-esteem.
- You can celebrate the successful meeting of an IEP target.
- You can celebrate any achievement, however small, that you feel needs public recognition, such as: 'Well done for cleaning out the hamster.'
- You can use school-based desk top publishing to make them specific to your school.
- They can go on a classroom wall, onto the board in the front entrance hall or into a ROA (record of achievement) – or all three.
- You can laminate them and send them home.
- You can give a certificate as a reward for completing a target-sheet.

Any child will be eligible for a certificate, so whilst you can use certificates to reward the meeting of an IEP target you will not be singling a child out unnecessarily. You will be using your usual classroom practice, but with a special focus. Certificates are available from LDA.

Ways for a child to celebrate their own achievement

This is most important. If we want a child to feel good about themself they must learn to be pleased with their own work or behaviour, and not rely on us telling them it is good.

Our ambition must be to move a child from:

> *'Look at that stupid kid over there, they can't even play football!', and going up to the child and mocking them, thereby making the critic feel better by stealing someone else's self-esteem and bumping up their own flagging reserves.*

Through:

> *'Look at that kid over there, they can't even play football! If I go over and play with him while Miss can see me, she'll see how kind I'm being and be nice to me', thereby bumping up self-esteem by attracting praise and public acclaim.*

To:

> *'Look at that kid over there, they can't even play football! I'll go and teach them some skills', and getting a bit of a buzz from the way the other child smiles and thanks their helper.*

The critic has become a hero who is prepared to help someone else.

So how do we get from stage 2 to stage 3 of this example?

> ● We must provide the child with a forum for celebrating their own achievement. A notice board with a large sign in the middle that simply says, 'This is my work and I'm proud of it' can be very helpful. Encourage the children to put work they are pleased with up on the board with no reference to the teacher. It is important that if they decide it is good, then that is good enough. This board won't have everything double

mounted or looking fancy or even straight, but it will show the beginnings of a child's capacity to validate their own work.

○ Once every couple of weeks or so, sit down with the child and their IEP book and look at the targets together. Ask them how they think they are doing. Let them decide. If you don't agree that they are doing better, don't say, 'Oh no, you're not. You are still not being kind to others' or whatever; they will not become kinder on hearing that, but simply become deaf to you. It really is important that they decide how they are doing for themself, just occasionally.

The 'I ...' stickers include:

○ I like noticing the good in others
○ I can join in well with other people
○ I can concentrate really well
○ I have been honest
○ I am patient
○ I have great looking skills
○ I want to make a change for the better
○ I have great listening skills
○ I have clear speaking skills
○ I have great thinking skills

These are all also excellent stickers to slap on a child's jumper whenever you catch them being good.

You can also make use of a packet of sticky red dots:

○ Give the child five red dots each week. Tell them they can affix one to each piece of work they are pleased with. Tell them they do not have to ask you if the work is good enough; if they are pleased with it, that is fine. I have known a child want to stay behind – 'Because I want to finish this work, Miss. So I can red dot it.'

○ If you remind a child to use the red dots, even if only for the period of the IEP, you will have a record of the work they feel is good. This is also useful for their ROA.

Ways of letting parents know about a child's achievements

I think we have to accept that in schools and homes there are very few 'bad guys'. All too often when we have to try to help children with behavioural difficulties, we all end up blaming each other. We are, generally speaking, all of us – parents, carers and teachers – doing our best.

We must keep in mind that not all parents have good memories of school. The stories they have to tell of their years in school may well be stories of failure and even humiliation. When their own children go to school, they want them to do well. If they do, all is fine. If, on the other hand, they too have difficulties then this may invoke in a parent all their bad memories about school. All that sense of failure and humiliation comes back again. Moreover, who is bringing it back? One of the people they love most in the world, their own child.

If this is going to prove too painful to bear a second time, not surprisingly the parent may reject the school and everything it is doing to their family. School becomes a place full of the enemy.

Often, however, the school won't stop sending home bad news about the child. The parent has to go into school, see the teacher and have all their child's failures served up on a report, a SATS result, a stage 2 IEP, a green form, a pink form, a buff form and ultimately a statement.

By the time a child has got to stage 3, their parent is having to sign forms detailing all of this humiliation.

As teachers, we know a parent has to sign a stage 3 form so they will know who is working with their child and the nature of the child's problems. To a parent it can seem as if they are being asked to sign a confession of their own failure.

Let me first make the suggestion that before you get to the stage of having to write IEPs – and maybe to help prevent your ever having to do so – you should send home good news all the time.

Do this in as many ways as you can dream up:

- ○ Photocopy good work and send it home in a properly addressed envelope. Just think how nice it would be for a parent to open the post in the morning and find a letter that says, 'We are pleased to inform you that Jon can now do his 6, 7 and 9 times table.' Think what a good start that would be for Jon's morning and imagine the mood he would be in when he came into school.

- ○ After issuing certificates, go out at the end of the day and put them into the parents' hands, if they come to school, and smile at those parents warmly. If you don't usually see them, post the certificates. But make sure they arrive with style and ceremony!

- Make fridge magnets with the children (buy cheap magnets, use dough for the front) and send each home with a postcard with a cheerful message on it: 'I am pleased with the way Jon read in class/helped with the little ones/smiled at me' – whatever. That piece of good news will go straight onto the fridge where it will cheer up a family and cause Jon to be a source of pride, not pain.

- Make the occasional phone call home. 'Hello, this is Maria's school. Just to let you know she did her dance in assembly today, with the class, and it was wonderful! Ask her to tell you about it. You would have been so proud.'

- If you want to use merit sticker-books as a record of a child's achievement, that's fine, but if you stick a specific sticker on a child's jumper that is a good, quick way to send an encouraging message home.

- If the child is on a star chart for any reason and at the end of the week they have done well, send the chart home.

- Make it special if you know you are going to send it home. Make it look good and laminate it. I have known really successful star charts go home and be put in clip frames and hung on the wall.

- During a staff Circle Time have a round in which everyone tells the others the best way they have found to send good news home. Write them all down and circulate them.

If good news goes home regularly, from the time the child enters the school, it will mean the child has amassed a huge store of self-respect for their achievements and a wealth of parental pride. Should something go wrong, a bit of bad news will not break the bank.

6 Sharing the IEP

or

whose IEP is it anyway?

Once you have got some targets and strategies in place, it is very important that the child is aware of the entire contents of their IEP.

They are really not going to want to sit down with a buff-coloured form and try to work out what this is going to mean to how they behave in the classroom or whom they can wallop in the playground. But they are the one the whole thing applies to; it is their behaviour that is under discussion and their learning that is suffering (among others'). So, how can we be sure that they know what plans we have for them and how can they be reminded of them whenever they might be in danger of forgetting?

I suggest you have a little child-friendly book that they can fill in with their teacher, the SENCO, a classroom assistant or – if you are lucky enough to have any – the stage 3 behaviour support teacher. Keep the whole thing together with a slide binder.

- This book, as well as designing, implementing and tracking the IEP, would also help promote cooperation between home and school.
- As well as the pages filled out in school, with the help of the staff mentioned above, there would also be the chance to include any completed target-sheets or ladders of achievement.
- Photocopies of good work could go in, as well as going home.

- If you have a Circle Time for the child you can include the list of suggestions and offers of help made by the rest of the class.
- A duplicate copy of special certificates could go in.
- There could be a record of lost Golden Time if this proves to be a list showing improvement.
- There could be spaces for messages from home to school or school to home.

This should be a **positive** record that will reflect the successes of the intervention and record the TATTs and the dates when they were achieved. When it comes to a review of the IEP, there should be abundant material to use, gained in a manageable manner with the full cooperation and knowledge of the child and parents concerned.

Photocopiable sheets to include in this record are supplied on the following pages.

Me

This is me:

And this is
my school:

This is my name: _____

This is my class: _____

welcome to the book about me.

There are some things in school I am really BRILLIANT at!
I am really good at:

We do many exciting things in school. Sometimes we go on outings. We also have our own assemblies and concerts and plays. Sometimes we play games with other schools. I am looking forward to:

1

2

3

4

I have got some friends in school. My friends are:

Our best playground games are:

Sometimes I get worried at school. I worry about:

1

2

3

The people who look after me at home worry about me too.
They care for me. That is why they worry. They worry about:

Sometimes my teachers worry about me. They care for me as
well. The things that concern them most about me are:

In our class we sometimes talk about things that worry us.
We sit together and help each other sort out our problems.
We do this in Circle Time. I should like to have a Circle Time
about some of my problems. I should like to see if people can
help me with:

In my school we have Golden Rules.

These are:

Do be gentle	–	Don't hurt anybody
Do be kind and helpful	–	Don't hurt people's feelings
Do listen	–	Don't interrupt
Do work hard	–	Don't waste your or other people's time
Do look after property	–	Don't waste or damage it
Do be honest	–	Don't cover up the truth

We also have Golden Time.

My favourite Golden Time activities are:

1

2

3

My favourite Circle Time games are:

1

2

3

Sometimes I need to work a little bit harder at some of the Golden Rules.

We talk about the Golden Rules in Circle Time.

At the moment I am trying especially hard with the following Golden Rules:

My teacher says these are my **aims**. I am aiming to be able to keep these rules really well.

I will have to learn how to keep these rules by moving towards them in small steps. These small steps towards my **aims** are called **targets**.

My targets are:

1

2

3

It is very difficult to change how you behave.

During a Circle Time my teachers and my class thought up some special ways to help me. Everyone offered to help me.

The suggestions I liked best were:

1	
2	
3	

These are called **strategies**.

Here are some of the other ways in which the teachers are going to help me:

1	
2	
3	

I have been given lots of stickers. I have taken them home. The words on them are important. Here are the words on some of my stickers and the dates when I was given them:

Words on sticker:	Date:

I have been given some certificates too. Below is a list of some of the things I have had certificates for and the dates when I was given them:

Certificate:	Date:

Some of these certificates are photocopied and put in this book. These help me see how I am getting along with my small steps towards my aim.

Along the way I have had some prizes. The best were:

Prize:	Date:

The important role of midday supervisors

or

you can run but you can't hide!

When writing an IEP it is very important to remember that one-sixth of a child's school day is spent under the jurisdiction of the lunchtime supervisors, otherwise known as the midday supervisory assistants (MDSAs) or school meal supervisory assistants (SMSAs).

Being an MDSA can be a truly miserable job. They are thrown into an often cold, windswept concrete yard with huge numbers of children per adult, for what seems like an interminable amount of time. They are frequently given no status, no equipment and no training and they receive terrible pay. What is more, although they are usually employed for only one and a half hours a day, that completely breaks up their day.

Frequently MDSAs have no access to the usual school sanction system. When faced with having to arbitrate between innumerable different quarrels a day, as well as having to break up fights and sort out the bullied from the bullies, it is not surprising that many MDSAs loathe the aggressive boys and the petulant, argumentative girls, preferring to walk around holding the hands of the younger, more amenable children.

It's not surprising, but it's not helpful to the child on an IEP.

First, I suggest some of the ideas in Chapter 1, in the 'Lunchtimes' section on pp. 9–11, are tried out in the school.

Then I think it is useful to consider how you are going to ensure that all the good work you are doing with the child and their IEP in the classroom is carried over into lunchtimes. You may like to consider some of the following ideas:

- Ensure that the MDSAs know how the whole model works, and know about its practical application. You can either encourage them to come to training days or you can give them some paid training time and train them yourself. Giving high quality training is a good way to show valuable people that they are appreciated.

- Ensure the MDSAs receive training in the rewards and sanctions available, and in the practical use of praise. Make sure they have their own supply of certificates, pin-on badges and stickers.

- Put up good, big, durable signs in the playground with the Golden Rules prominently displayed on them. The MDSAs will then be able to use the same words as the rest of the staff to praise or reprimand a child.

- Discuss 'Catch them being good – blink and you'll miss it' with the lunchtime staff.

- Give ideas for rewards and incentives, such as 'Table of the Week', or give the MDSAs their own notice board in the dining hall on which photographs of 'Lunchtime Stars of the Week' can be displayed.

IEPs, lunchtimes and lunchtime staff

Here are some ideas for involving MDSAs in the IEP:

- When writing the IEP it is useful to put in some aims, targets and strategies for lunchtime behaviour. Few children who are having any kind of difficulty with their behaviour rush joyfully into the playground and behave like children in a Kate Greenaway illustration. Ensuring that your IEP is consistent throughout the entire day will make it much more effective.

- Give a copy of the IEPs to the senior MDSA. Try to find a few minutes to talk these over with them. Very often MDSAs feel that no one is sharing a child's management plan with them, and yet they are outside trying to manage that child day after day. If we have a plan for a child, we must share it with all of those concerned with the child's welfare and behaviour, and that must include the lunchtime staff.

◗ The senior MDSA will then be able to speak with the rest of their team about any plans or strategies. Very often MDSAs feel isolated from the rest of the school staff. They often say, 'They don't tell us anything. We never know what's going on.' They shouldn't feel like this – they are school staff too.

Ensure each supervisor has two little booklets. One will have pages that look like this:

To ....

I am pleased with you because ....

Signed ....

The other will have pages that say:

To ....

I am disappointed in you because ....

Signed ....

Examples of similar booklets are included in *Photocopiable Materials for use with the Jenny Mosley Circle Time Model*, details of which can be found in the Resources at the back of this book. The point of these booklets is that they enable an MDSA to write down anything they need to communicate to the class teacher of a child with, or without, an IEP.

If it is a positive remark, the MDSA can give it to the child and ask that they hand it to their class teacher. If it is an 'I am disappointed ...' slip, the MDSA can hand that directly to the class teacher at the end of the lunchtime break.

The advantage of this system is that the teacher can then tell the child they will discuss the contents of the note at a point in the afternoon which is convenient to the teacher. The child is not hijacking the start of the afternoon with endless debate about what they did or didn't do, and whose fault it was. The teacher can put the note in their pocket and say, 'We will discuss this later; now let's get on with the afternoon.'

It is important that the class teacher always takes one minute off a child's Golden Time every time they receive a 'Disappointed' slip from an MDSA. This should be done even if the teacher is unsure about the nature or severity of the misdeed. By respecting the MDSA's judgement and using the sanction system that operates in the classroom to support the MDSA, the class teacher is ensuring that the MDSA has proper status as a member of the staff team.

This demonstrates to the child that wherever they are the rules and the sanctions are the same. It also makes it clear that lunchtimes are part of the normal school day: 'You can run but you can't hide.'

If the misdemeanour is serious the class teacher could, of course, remove more than one minute from the child's Golden Time.

Ensure that the MDSA knows which targets can be rewarded with specific stickers, and that they have these stickers to hand. After a few good days a certificate might be issued. Lunchtime certificates must carry the same weight as those issued in class.

Once the MDSA has a copy of the IEPs and a way of informing the class teacher about a child's behaviour, good and bad, and of rewarding good playtime behaviour, it can be said that the plan is reasonably comprehensive.

You will also have demonstrated to the other children that you recognise and understand that this particular child has problematic playtime behaviour, and that this is being addressed. Often children are frightened by one child's wild behaviour in the playground and feel that it is going relatively unchecked. This impression can go home to parents, who are then under the mistaken impression that 'Nothing is being done about ...'s behaviour.'

If the MDSAs have access to a system such as is outlined above, all the children can see that good and bad behaviour is recognised and noted, and co-ordinated action is taken. When a child loses Golden Time because of playtime behaviour the other children know that all the staff communicate with each other. This will help nervous children feel more secure and may deter those who are considering a life of crime in the playground.

Moreover if you do not attempt to include lunchtimes in the plan, you will often find that things go wrong at lunchtime and a good morning can be followed by an awful afternoon. That can make it tempting to keep the child in at lunchtime. This is dreadfully inconvenient for the class teacher and is not really teaching the child how to manage their playtime behaviour. And playtime behaviour may be something they most need to learn to manage.

What is more, if things have been improving in the morning, you don't want to lose the momentum of this good work. Keeping the child under the same umbrella of rules, targets, rewards and sanctions through a comprehensive lunchtime plan should increase the chances of the child returning to the classroom in the afternoon in a state of mind not too different from that of the morning.

8 Desperate cases – desperate measures

or

daily Golden Time as a strategy

There will be children whose behaviour is so difficult that you will decide you are on the verge of permanently excluding them. You may feel that you don't want to do this, but that you cannot contain them any longer.

If they were to be excluded, they might be found a place at another school – however, you may know that they have finally exhausted that possibility. They would possibly go to a special EBD school or, if a place could not be found, maybe go onto home tuition.

If you are facing these possibilities, then I suggest you put the child onto a very tight schedule of targets and rewards.

Let us imagine this is a plan for a child who will not do as they are asked. They disturb the work of the other children in the class and often fight and bully other children in the playground. When you ask them to sit down they refuse, they answer back very rudely when you speak to them and they skip off to the other side of the room when you go towards them. They will swear at you and laugh in your face. They do exactly as they like from 9 a.m. to 3.30 p.m. and if they do as you ask, it is only because that happens to suit them at the time.

Before I outline the plan for a child such as this, I must say it is going to take some additional support if it is to work. By this I mean you will need to have the guaranteed support of a classroom assistant, welfare support or teacher for fifteen minutes every afternoon. It is inappropriate for a parent helper to assist with this.

You will also need somewhere quiet to go for these fifteen minutes. It may have to be the headteacher's office if your school is small or full.

Given that we have borrowed a classroom assistant or someone else for fifteen minutes towards the end of the afternoon, what are we to do?

- ❍ First set the child – let us call them Marvin – two straightforward targets, one for work and one for social relations. There are two outlined in the sample IEP at the end of this chapter; see pp. 82–3.
- ❍ You will need a chart, which may look like this:

Time	Work	Behaviour
9–10		
10–11		
11–12		
12–1		
1–2		
2–3		

Laminate this chart, or cover it with sticky backed plastic, so you can mark it with a dry wipe pen and use the same chart every day for weeks.

- ❍ The essence of this particular plan is that you divide the day up into hour segments.
- ❍ At the end of each hour the teacher decides if Marvin has worked satisfactorily and if he has behaved satisfactorily. The teacher may ask him how he feels he has done, but if there is disagreement about the behaviour the teacher's decision is final. There is no time for lengthy discussion and negotiation is not to be recommended.
- ❍ If the teacher feels Marvin has worked well, he can have a tick under **Work**.
- ❍ If he has behaved well, he can have a tick under **Behaviour**.

- Marvin may end up with just one tick or two, or with none. If he has not gained a tick he gets a dash.
- There is no need for rancour when ticking the chart. It should be a quick matter-of-fact assessment in which Marvin is with you and his results are recorded.
- At the end of the day, he has a maximum of twelve ticks.
- For each tick, he keeps a minute of his special Golden Time.
- This means that if he is to have fifteen minutes of his own special Golden Time, he will have three minutes' guaranteed time and twelve minutes that he may lose.
- At the end of the day add up the number of dashes. The total is the number of minutes he has lost.

How to organise Golden Time

Continuing the example of Marvin:

- First take him into a quiet office with his class teacher, the SENCO and the headteacher. In a very small school these may well be one person. If that is the case, ask another member of staff to be with you to take notes.
- Tell Marvin that he is going to be given a special programme to follow for half a term or maybe a term. Explain that he will enjoy this and that the more his behaviour improves, the nicer the rewards he will get.
- Tell him he is going to have fifteen minutes every day of his own special Golden Time.
- During this time activities that he has chosen will be available. These will be things he really likes.
- As with ordinary Golden Time, if he misbehaves he will lose this time – except for the last three minutes, which he will always have.
- Tell him he will have a special box with his Golden Time activities in it; these could include computer games if there is a computer he can use. These activities will only be available during his special Golden Time.
- Ask him what he would really like to do. Note this down.
- Try hard to accommodate him. He has got to make a huge

change in his behaviour. He really has got to feel it is worth the effort.

How to make this plan acceptable to the other children

We do not want the other children to feel their good behaviour is a disadvantage to them. Here are some suggestions for achieving this:

- Tell the class about the special Golden Time.
- Tell them that you will be selecting one child each day to play with Marvin. The child you select will be someone who has worked very hard and tried to behave well all day.
- This will help turn Marvin into a prize, not a torture, in the eyes of his classmates.
- Try to select a good cross-section of children as the days go on. It won't work if it is always the same child, Marvin's friend or a child of the same sex.

What to do at 3 o'clock

It is important to organise this fully. Here is the procedure:

- At 3 p.m., when the person who is helping you arrives, tell them how many minutes Marvin has lost. The accompanying child may have lost Golden Time that day, but they will settle their debts at the same time as the rest of the class during the regular class Golden Time.
- The three of them – two children and one helper – go off with the special Golden Time box.
- When they get to the room, library corner, deputy head's office or wherever, usual Golden Time rules apply.
- An activity selected by Marvin is taken out of the box.
- He has to sit quietly, with a clock or timer, for the number of minutes he has lost.
- The other two are not to talk to him, harangue him or in any way entertain him during this time. Just let him sit and watch the minutes slowly pass.

- The accompanying child can start to play straight away.
- If Marvin misbehaves, the helper tells him the time does not start until he is sitting quietly.
- If he misbehaves throughout the first twelve minutes, he still is allowed the last three. If he does not have these he will not know how nice it can be to have his special Golden Time. He may also feel hard done by and expect never to get any time. This would defeat the object of special Golden Time.

To make this work really well you must remember:

- Fill the chart in at the end of each hour, promptly.
- Do not get into any kind of negotiation over time lost. Many children are brilliant at pushing the boundaries and have been doing it successfully for years. If you let Marvin spoil this system by allowing yourself to be bullied into giving him time he does not deserve, you are not doing him any favours. If he doesn't deserve a tick, he doesn't get it. After all, it's only one minute you are depriving him of, not three weeks' playtime. If he complains, tell him nicely that he can always try a bit harder for the next hour.
- If he says he doesn't care, he doesn't want any Golden Time anyway, don't be drawn into a discussion or argument. Just go on giving him the fair amount of ticks and dashes. At the end of the day send him off for his special time. You are in charge of this system, not him. If you let him hijack it (which he may well try to do), it is not fair on him.
- As long as the activities are things Marvin really enjoys and you never fail to provide the special Golden Time at the same time, every day, as expected, he will gradually change his behaviour to get more time.
- It may take half a term or even longer to see good, consistent results. It has taken a long time for things to get as bad as they are – they won't get better in a fortnight.
- Be utterly reliable in your time-keeping during Golden Time. If Marvin has only got four minutes, then he has only got four minutes. If you are casual with your time-keeping, it won't work as well as it might.
- Don't start this system until you know you can run it consistently and reliably. If you start it, mismanage it, drop it

and then try again next term, he will not believe you are as good as your word – and it won't work! Think of it as like taking antibiotics; if you don't do that properly, eventually they don't work, and then you are in deep trouble.

Putting special Golden Time onto an IEP

You might want to include:

Aims:

▷ We would like Marvin to settle quickly to the work set.

 GOLDEN RULE – DO WORK HARD.
DON'T WASTE YOUR OR OTHER PEOPLE'S TIME.

▷ We would like Marvin to speak politely to his teacher and classmates.

 GOLDEN RULES – DO BE GENTLE. DON'T HURT ANYBODY.
DO BE KIND. DON'T HURT PEOPLE'S FEELINGS.

Targets:

❍ Marvin is to follow the direction of his teacher, and is to settle to work, or follow any other instructions given during the hour, within three minutes. (This can be reduced incrementally if you wish.)

❍ Marvin is not to swear, speak abusively to others or be violent during the hour.

❍ Marvin is to try to achieve eight or more minutes' special Golden Time, out of the maximum of twelve, for four consecutive days by two weeks before the end of term.

Strategies:

- Marvin will have his day divided into hourly target segments.
- He will be monitored every hour.
- He will be given fifteen minutes' Golden Time a day. Twelve of these minutes are dependent upon meeting his targets. He will lose one minute of his Golden Time for each missed target.
- All of the time gained will be recorded in his personal IEP book, 'All about me'. (See Chapter 6, pp. 65.)
- As well as the special Golden Time, Marvin is to have his successes acknowledged through the award of certificates. Provided he has not lost more than fifty minutes' Golden Time in a week, a certificate is to go to his home celebrating his efforts and achievement. (You could incrementally increase the amount of time needed to gain a certificate, e.g. in week 2 he must have not lost more than forty-five minutes.)
- Marvin is to be asked if he would like to borrow one of the pin-on target badges for some period of each day.
- MDSAs are to be informed of this plan and to tell his class teacher how well he has managed the time in the playground.
- All staff are to praise and acknowledge any good behaviour spotted throughout the day. (Even if it is suspected that he was only behaving well accidentally!)
- If he meets his target of managing eight or more minutes' special Golden Time out of the maximum of twelve for four consecutive days by two weeks before the end of term, he can have … (Choose something he would like; helping the caretaker for an hour, acting as the secretary's runner for a morning, answering the school phone over lunchtime – whatever he would like that is appropriate.)

Review Marvin's progress after six weeks. Keep his personal IEP book up to date and bring it to the review.

This plan is really only to be used in exceptional circumstances as it is very labour intensive. However, there are occasions when we all know that if we don't do something drastic we are going to have to exclude a child permanently. If we feel permanent exclusion is right, that's fine. If we would really rather not exclude a child, we could always try this system.

Individual Education Plan   No: 4

> Pupil's Name: Marvin Odone   Class: 7N   N.C. Year: 7
>
> Code of Practice Stage: 1 2 3 ④ 5 (Please circle)   Date: 1.3.98

Concerns

1. Marvin will not do as he is asked.
2. He disturbs the work of the other children in the class and often fights and bullies other children in the playground.
3. When asked to sit down he refuses.
4. Marvin answers back rudely when you speak to him and he skips off to the other side of the room when you go towards him.
5. Marvin will swear at you and laughs in peoples faces.

General aims of provision planned

1. We would like Marvin to settle quickly to the work set.

 **GOLDEN RULE – DO WORK HARD.
DON'T WASTE YOUR OR OTHER PEOPLE'S TIME.**

2. We would like Marvin to speak politely to his teacher and classmates.

 **GOLDEN RULES – DO BE GENTLE. DON'T HURT ANYBODY.
DO BE KIND. DON'T HURT PEOPLE'S FEELINGS.**

Specific targets

Marvin is to follow the daily Golden Time ticks and targets routine. (See Chapter 8.)

1. Marvin is to follow the direction of his teacher to settle to work, or follow any other instructions given during the hour, within 3 minutes (decreasing incrementally if you wish).
2. Marvin is not to swear, speak abusively to others or be violent during each of these hour periods.
3. Marvin is to try to manage 8 or more minutes out of the 12 possible Golden Time minutes, for 4 consecutive days by 2 weeks before the end of term.

Strategies to be used

1. Marvin will have his day divided into hourly target segments.

2. He will be monitored hour on hour.

3. He will be given 15 minutes' Golden Time a day. Twelve of these minutes are dependent upon his meeting his targets. He will lose 1 minute of his Golden Time for each missed target.

4. All of the time gained will be recorded in his personal IEP book, 'All about me'. (See Chapter 6, pp. 65.)

5. As well as the special Golden Time, Marvin is to have his successes acknowledged through the award of certificates. Provided he has not lost more than 50 minutes' Golden Time in a week, a certificate is to go to his home celebrating his efforts and achievement. (We will incrementally increase the amount of time needed to gain a certificate, e.g. in week 2 he must have not lost more than 45 minutes.)

6. Marvin is to be asked if he would like to borrow one of the pin-on target badges for some period of each day.

7. MDSAs are to be informed of this plan and to tell his class teacher how well he has managed the time in the playground.

8. All staff are to praise and acknowledge any good behaviour spotted throughout the day (even if it is suspected that he was only behaving well accidentally!).

9. If he reaches his target of managing 8 or more minutes out of the 12 for 4 consecutive days by 2 weeks before the end of term, he can have something he would like – helping the caretaker for an hour, acting as the secretary's runner for a morning, answering the school phone over lunchtime; whatever he would like that is appropriate. Ask him.

Review

After 6 weeks. Keep his personal IEP book up to date and bring it to the review.

9 Special needs Circle Times

When I first heard about the idea of special needs Circle Times, I have to admit I felt uncomfortable. I could not imagine that children who had an assortment of problems with their learning and behaviour would want to meet together to discuss these disparate difficulties.

After a while I realised that was very patronising of me. What I was essentially saying was, 'You have difficulties with reading, you with making friends and you with fighting; I am sure you wouldn't want other people to know about these problems.' But they do want to talk together in a Circle Time. That is precisely the point of Circle Time. They are not ashamed of these difficulties, they just want to get them fixed.

Before discussing special needs Circle Time, I will first tell you about a little girl called Hannah – a real girl with real problems, but this is not her real name.

Hannah had had a troubled life, despite being only 9 years old. She had lost touch with her real father, who had been violent, and her 'new' father was in prison for GBH. As a result of many difficult years, Hannah's mother had had a nervous breakdown and was in hospital. Hannah and her little sister lived with foster carers. While her mother was in hospital, her second father came out of prison and threatened to take her away, although he was not supposed to have custody of her. He became violent at her school one day and smashed the windows of some teachers' cars. Hannah knew all that was going on. She was, naturally enough, very frightened.

Hannah had a Statement; she had been diagnosed as dispraxic some years before and, in addition, had difficulties both with her academic work and with making friends. She had a full-time learning assistant as a provision of the statement.

In class Hannah would not do work she found even remotely difficult; she would just fold her arms across her chest and say, 'I can't do this.' Her learning assistant was becoming worn out.

Hannah would often speak in a strange voice, as if she didn't want to speak in her own voice. Unsurprisingly, Hannah was not keen on being herself. On Maslow's hierarchy of needs Hannah could not even make the second rung.

The trouble was we could not do anything about her situation. We could not make Hannah safe. We could not even kid her into believing she was safe in school; she wasn't entirely, and she knew it.

The EP did some tests with her. During these tests it become obvious that she was excessively concerned about children being killed or murdered. She was negative in her remarks about men. Hannah loved her mother, her grandfather and her sister dearly, but she was powerless to put her family back together again. We all felt pretty powerless as well. But we had to help her. We were faced with what is all too often the teacher's problem – responsibility but so little power.

Hannah had effectively come to a dead stop. She would not work, she wasn't learning, she would not even speak in her normal voice, she would not unfold her arms from across her chest. We had to have a meeting to write her new IEP.

We would like to have said that our aims were to put Hannah's family back together, to restore her lost childhood, to help her see that it was summer and that the wind was warm and there were clouds of butterflies sweeping over the water-meadows.

And I suppose in a way that was our aim, except that because we were grown-up people we recognised that we could do none of that. The best thing we could do was help Hannah grow up with self-confidence and strength that would empower her to do those things for herself. We knew that she had to find her own way to the water-meadows.

So instead we wrote:

Aims:

(1) We would like Hannah to feel that she can make good things happen in her life, that she can be pro-active.

 GOLDEN RULE – DO BE KIND AND HELPFUL.

② We would like Hannah to go from saying 'I can't' to saying 'I'll try.'

 GOLDEN RULE – DO WORK HARD.

③ We would like Hannah to see that men can be relied on to be gentle and able to guide her behaviour without being in any way violent.

 GOLDEN RULE – DO BE GENTLE.

Targets:

● We were going to look for at least one situation every day in which Hannah could be of help to another child. If Hannah was to feel that she was able to make good things happen, it wouldn't help if she thought we were 'arranging' this. I think she might have guessed that she wasn't quite as powerful as she imagined. We wanted her to feel that she was a 'good fairy', but we recognised that we would have to offer an unseen guiding hand.

● Hannah was to complete one task a day with her learning assistant. This task would start by being a three-minute task and go up to become a ten-minute task by the end of the term.

● Hannah would be able to accept Al, one of the male learning assistants, as her afternoon helper by the end of the term. She would start by just having him help her for one lesson a week; the time would progressively increase to every afternoon.

● She was to be able to tell us one nice thing that she and Al had done in each lesson.

Strategies:

● We would hold a class Circle Time, 'I find it easier to work when ...'.

● We would steer Hannah towards situations where she could be of help.

- When she did make something happen that was beneficial to herself or others, we had to be sure to leap in and praise her.
- We had to get her to acknowledge her success and, if possible, have other children recognise it too.
- She would be given specific stickers, such as, 'We like the way you are a good friend' and 'Thank you for being kind/helpful.'
- We were to use words which would make it clear to Hannah that she had been pro-active, for example, 'Well done, Hannah, for comforting Jo when she was crying. She feels a great deal better now, and all because of you. You are a kind girl'; or 'Well done, Hannah, for seeing that Jack was going to need the sellotape and finding it. He has finished his model now, thanks to you. You are kind and helpful.'
- We would ask her to tell us all about it so she could relate what had prompted her thoughtfulness. She never realised that many of the situations were initially a set-up. In the case of Jo, we had led her over to the situation. Often we diverted others who might have been more prompt with help away from a situation. We decided that if she felt she could make things better, she might eventually feel more in control and thus a little safer.
- When Hannah folds her arms and says, 'I can't', we need to use that as a signal to say, 'What can we do and what can you do that is going to help you say, "I'll try"?'
- Each time she completed a task in line with a target, she would get a flower on her chart. (We used the flower target sheet, *Photocopiable Materials*, pp. 31–2; see the Resources list.)
- If she would not work, then she was breaking the Golden Rule: 'Do work hard – Do not waste your or other people's time' and, after a warning, she would lose a minute of her Golden Time.

At the end we added another strategy to the IEP: Hannah was to be invited to the special needs Circle Time each week.

There were no strategies needed for Al. He was one of the kindest and most sensitive men. She was happy to work with him. We just had to keep pointing out to her how kind he was!

The special needs Circle Time

In order to find some customers for our special needs Circle Time, we decided to go through the special needs register and invite any child at stage 3, 4 or 5 whom we felt had emotional or behavioural difficulties that were adversely affecting their learning. We also asked the rest of the staff for candidates.

This amounted to about fifteen children from across all four of the middle school years, 4–7.

We sent out invitations which we photocopied from *Photocopiable Materials* by Jenny Mosley.

On the first day we were anxious. Would any of them turn up? They did! With one exception, all of the children invited came.

What did we do?

Week 1:

Once we were all in the circle, Karen very gently welcomed everyone and said how pleased she was to see each of the people in the circle. We did not need to go over the Circle Time rules as all the children in the school regularly had Circle Time as part of their timetable and were quite familiar with the ground rules.

She then, very bravely but honestly, said:

> *'I am sure you all realise that we have invited you today because each of you has experienced difficulties in school, of one kind or another, and we want to see if we can sort out some of these problems through these special Circle Times.'*

I have to say I was waiting to see what would be said at this point. However, the children merely nodded sensibly.

The script for the first session was very easy:

- ❍ We played a game – peach, pear, plum – which meant we had to swap seats with each other.
- ❍ Then we had a simple round of introducing ourselves and telling the group about something that we liked doing.
- ❍ We then played another game and had a round of thank yous.

This last was difficult as most of the children did not come into contact with each other through the week, but we managed two or three thank yous, which meant we finished on a positive note.

> ❍ Karen then asked everyone to come again the next week, and this time to bring along a photograph that was important to them.

Week 2:

The next week Karen again sent out invitations to the children, and again the children arrived, each with a photograph. We followed the usual script:

> ❍ The round was quite simply, 'Tell us about your photograph and why it's important to you.'

The children told us all about past holidays, favourite nannas, loved pets. One by one in the circle, each spoke and everyone else listened intently and respectfully.

> ❍ At the close of the session Karen asked if the following week they could bring something that was important to them.

Week 3:

Week 3 was even better. For one thing, we had a few attempted gatecrashers. They said they had heard how these Circle Times were really good and asked if they could come along. Lesley, the SENCO, had to say, very nicely, to them that unfortunately this Circle Time was strictly by invitation only. The attempts to join in were gratifying as it meant the usual participants must have been giving us a good press.

The Circle Time itself went well. The things the children had brought rather took our breath away. As well as some special teddies and an assortment of other cuddly toys and comfort blankets, we also had a large hamster that appeared out of a boy's pocket and a jar that came out from under a chair and contained a selection of stick insects!

> ❍ All the children were asked to say what was important to them about each of the things they had brought.
> ❍ For the following session they were asked to bring a **person** who meant a great deal to them.

No one could say we were not brave!

Week 4:

By now our special Circle Time was beginning to mean a great deal to each of us. It was entirely non-threatening and it was not a time of great introspection. It did not take up a vast amount of time; it ran from 12.40 to 1.00 p.m. during lunchtime.

However, it was a time when everyone was listened to, and so we were beginning to build up a great deal of trust.

When the Circle Time on the fourth week opened we knew we had caused something rather powerful to happen.

Children had brought their learning assistant, their favourite MDSA, their younger siblings from the first school downstairs; someone had brought the headteacher. Hannah had brought her grandfather.

There was also one extra child. During another Circle Time in the previous week I had seen her cry when she spoke. She said she felt people were laughing at her and she did not have any friends. After that Circle Time I asked her if she wanted to come along to the special Circle Time, and she said she would.

- ❍ We welcomed everyone to Circle Time.
- ❍ We then briefly outlined the script and played a quick game. The entire group joined in and we played 'Electric squeeze'. (You hold hands with the person on either side of you and a gentle squeeze is passed around the group. It's a simple game and always popular.)
- ❍ After this we had a round in which each person had to say why they brought the person they had chosen with them, if they were a chooser. The people who had been brought had to say how they felt to have been chosen.
- ❍ Everyone was allowed only one or two sentences, but it was very moving. Children said, quite simply, how the people they had brought helped them or made them feel good about themselves or always listened to them or were just their friend. The people who had been brought said they felt very pleased to have been chosen. Some said they had not realised until then how much they meant to their chooser.
- ❍ Hannah said she had brought her grandfather because she loved him and he was always kind to her. He said he was grateful to Hannah for having brought him as he was glad of the chance to share a Circle Time. He said it meant a great deal to him that Hannah had said he was kind to her

and that she had made him very happy. We could have kissed him – but of course we didn't.

○ We then talked about how nice it was to have a special person whom we could trust, whom we knew would listen if we talked to them and wouldn't tell everyone what was worrying us. I asked everyone, children and adults, to think for a moment of the person whom they trusted the most. I then said at some stage during the coming week we were to tell that person that we trusted them.

Week 5:

This week we had a large circle. All of the staff who were at last week's circle, including the headteacher, came along, as well as the usual invitees.

After a game we had a round.

○ I asked people to say if they had told the person whom they trusted of their trust.

We promptly had a crisis. One of the girls burst into tears and said that she had wanted to tell her grandma that she trusted her but that she had died two days after the previous Circle Time. She was very distressed, so we asked her if she would like to go outside and talk to a teacher about this on her own and she said she would.

○ We went round the circle and everyone briefly said what had happened when they told people they trusted them. Some people had found it easier to do than others, but they were all glad they had done it.

○ The girl who had cried in the class circle had been told by another girl in the circle, who was also in her class, that she was her trusted friend. This had pleased her enormously.

○ Hannah had told her grandfather that she had trusted him and as she had also brought him along to the school we felt she was beginning to take some charge of her own emotional life. We had no idea how much we had underestimated her.

This last Circle Time had taken place during the penultimate week of term. I was not supposed to be going back into the school again that term. However, two days before the end of term I received a phone call from Lesley, the SENCO. Hannah had visited her in the special needs room and asked if she could have her own circle.

Lesley said, 'Yes.' But she confessed she did not know exactly what Hannah meant by this. Hannah replied, 'Don't worry, I can sort it out myself, but I need you to ask Mrs Goldthorpe.'

Hannah asked us all to be in school for Friday lunchtime. None of us knew quite what to expect, although it seemed likely Hannah had just wanted one last special Circle Time.

On Friday lunchtime I arrived. The corridor outside the special needs room appeared to be full of people, twenty at least – adults, children, strangers, familiar faces – all milling around in a confused way. Suddenly Hannah arrived and, in a calm manner, said, 'You are all here, good. You are all here for my Circle Time.'

It is very hard to explain how I felt at this minute or for the next twenty-five minutes. The feeling was a mixture of terrific elation, because I was aware I was present at an event which was one of the most remarkable of my life; and of the slightly fantastic, as if I were dreaming – but knew I wasn't. I imagine that being told you have won a great deal of money probably carries with it the same kind of feeling.

We all crowded into the special needs room and more chairs were fetched as the numbers were counted.

There were twenty-four people. There were a few of Hannah's classmates; some children from the infant school, including her sister; and some children from the special circle. There were an equal number of adults, including her learning assistant, her favourite MDSAs, the headteacher and one or two of her favourite members of staff. Her grandfather was there and so, looking tired and nervous, was her foster mother.

There was also her mother. It was the presence of her mother that lent an air of fable to the moment, giving the feeling of being in someone else's story. In real life very sick mothers don't leave hospital at the request of their 9-year-old daughters who, hitherto, have been incapable of action. They don't turn up dramatically at the last minute, so that the child not only realises how much their mother loves them but also realises that, even though they are only a child, they can act to help their parent.

All that belongs in a nineteenth-century novel or a late twentieth-century film – but this was real.

As we warmly welcomed Hannah's mother, who was plainly not well, and the other adults, and seated them as best we could in the circle, I felt an almost wearisome responsibility. For I realised that whilst, by the grace of God, we had been given the plot – a plot we could only have dreamed of – we had not so far been given the script.

What was to happen at this Circle Time was obviously very important and as we had had no idea what was going to take place, we had nothing whatsoever prepared.

Hannah knew what she wanted at the start of the Circle Time. She welcomed everyone in the warm and gentle way she had learned from the special circles, and then she asked everyone to introduce themself.

Everyone answered in the same way. Everyone said their name and their relationship to Hannah and finished with 'and I am Hannah's friend'.

As one person after another finished with 'and I am Hannah's friend' I realised the sense of something special, something that demanded ceremony, had affected all of us. As we went round the circle I was thinking rapidly. I felt fairly sure Hannah would have nothing further planned after this, and indeed when the introductions finished she turned to us and just smiled sweetly.

There were twenty-four people unexpectedly in front of us. All had come from busy lives, one at least was not well. They all were feeling the same sense of moment as we were. We had to make this into a special and worthwhile event.

I thought, 'Margaret, remember to stay with the circle script; it always works and you only need two sentences.'

I talked briefly about how sometimes we all feel that life is very difficult and we can't cope, and we may feel very apprehensive and unequal to the task in hand.

I then said we were each going to start a sentence with, 'I feel worried or apprehensive when ...'.

Everyone told the group something that made them feel either worried or fear that they might not be able to cope. Hannah's foster mother said she had felt apprehensive when Hannah's mother had asked her to look after Hannah and her sister.

I then said that although people often looked very confident, it was clear that everyone felt very anxious about their responsibilities at some time.

I explained that we would now have a round when people would tell each other what they did to help themselves when they felt like this. The sentence would be, 'When I feel like this I find it helps if I ...'.

Everyone made a suggestion. Some said they went to a friend and said, 'Tell me something that I can do well, because I'm feeling hopeless right now.' Others said they made lists of things that they knew they had done well, some said they prayed for help and guidance, some said they wrote the problem down so they could see it more clearly. Many said they went to a friend or relative and asked them to listen to the problem and then talk about how it might best be solved.

At the end of this round it was clear that we all knew what it was like to feel overwhelmed by a difficulty. We each knew that this feeling did not mean we were inadequate, it just meant we were the same as everyone else. We also now knew many ways in which other people coped with this feeling and how they overcame it.

At the end of the Circle Time we had a round of thank yous. The biggest thank you went to Hannah, who had recognised that people close to her were experiencing difficulties and had found a way to help them – she had brought them to a Circle Time.

I left with two powerful feelings; one was that I had been present at something very special that was not likely to happen often in my life, and the other was a deep feeling of respect for Hannah. She really had learned how to make good things happen.

Why do I relate all of this in such detail in a book about IEPs? Because I think it is important to remember, when we sit down to make a plan which we hope will change a child's learning or behaviour, that we may do just that. We are rewriting that child's script for them. We are making a plan that will interfere with the course of their story. We know we have to do it because the existing story is not a happy one – otherwise we would have no concerns – but we must nevertheless be aware of what it may mean to take a hand in the plot of someone else's life.

Individual Education Plan   No: 5

Pupil's Name: Hannah Souter Class: 4R	N.C. Year: 4
Code of Practice Stage: 1 2 3 4 ⑤ (Please circle)	Date: 12.6.97

Concerns

1   In class Hannah will not do work she finds even remotely difficult. She crosses her arms across her chest and says, 'I won't.'
2   She often speaks in a strange voice.
3   She is often very anxious and says she feels as if she has no control over people or events in her life.

General aims of provision planned

1   We would like Hannah to feel she can make good things happen in her life, that she can be pro-active.

 GOLDEN RULE – DO BE KIND AND HELPFUL.

2   We would like Hannah to go from saying 'I can't' to saying 'I'll try.'

 GOLDEN RULE – DO WORK HARD.

3   We would like Hannah to see that men can be relied on to be gentle and able to guide her behaviour without being in any way violent.

 GOLDEN RULE – DO BE GENTLE.

Specific targets

1   We will look for at least one situation every day where Hannah can be of help to another child.
2   Hannah is to complete one task a day with her learning assistant. This task will start by being a 3-minute task and go up to a 10-minute task by the end of term.
3   Hannah will be able to accept Al, one of the male learning assistants, as her afternoon helper by the end of term. She will start by just having him help her for one lesson a week and the time will progressively increase to every afternoon.

4   She will be able to tell us one nice thing that she and Al have done each lesson.

Strategies to be used

1   We will hold a class Circle Time 'I find it easier to work when ....

2   We will steer Hannah towards situations where she can be of help.

3   When she does make something happen that is beneficial to herself or others we must be sure to leap in and praise her.

4   We must get her to acknowledge her success and, if possible, have other children recognise it too. She will be given specific stickers, e.g. 'We like the way you are a good friend', 'Thank you for being kind/helpful.'

5   We will use words which will make it clear to Hannah that she has been pro-active, e.g., 'Well done, Hannah, for comforting Jo when she was crying. She feels a great deal better now, and all because of you. You are a kind girl.' 'Well done, Hannah, for seeing that Jack was going to need the sellotape and finding it. He has finished his model now, thanks to you. You are kind and helpful.'

6   We will ask her to 'Tell us all about it' and she can relate what has prompted her thoughtfulness.

7   When Hannah folds her arms and says 'I can't' we will use that as a signal to say, 'What can we do and what can you do that is going to help you say, "I'll try"?' We will supply lots of suggestions, e.g., 'Would it help if you listened to me reading the instructions for the work?' The slightest sign of compliance or effort on her part is to be rewarded with praise.

8   Each time she completes a task as per target she will get a flower on her chart. We used the flower target-sheet from Photocopiable Materials for use with the Jenny Mosley Circle Time Model.

9   If she will not work, she is breaking the Golden Rule: 'Do work hard – Do not waste your or other people's time.' After a warning, she will lose a minute of her Golden Time.

10   Hannah is to be invited to the special needs Circle Time each week.

We were not to know that strategy 10 was to prove dramatic in its effect; see chapter 9.

Appendix 1 Photocopiable material

In this book some photocopiable material has been supplied for your use:

⊙ All about me – a booklet for individual children to complete; see pp. 65.

In addition there is:

The **Case Overview** which can be photocopied and pasted to the outside of the file. It helps you to know at a glance what is inside; who has replied to letters, who has sent reports and who needs chasing up.

It is designed to make the approaching visit of the E.P. less stressful!

The **Listen, Repeat, Return, Complete Sheet** which is double sided. The instructions are on one side and the chart on the other. This can be photocopied and handed out with the kitchen timer when needed. The use of this chart is explained on page 40.

Instructions for the 'Listen – Repeat – Return – Complete' technique

❶ The child stands in front of you. You make good eye contact and tell the child **exactly** what they have to do, such as, 'Find your geography folder and pencil case. Then work on the map of your journey to school. I have put the timer on for five minutes. Come back when it rings. Now what have you got to do?'

❷ The child has to repeat this back to you **exactly**.

❸ If they do not repeat it **exactly**, then you repeat the instructions and ask the child to repeat it back to you again. It may take them two or three attempts before they realise they must repeat your instructions exactly. Saying 'Go and do my map' is not good enough. They must be able to say, 'Get my geography folder and my pencil case. Carry on working on the map of my journey to school. I've got to come back when the timer rings in five minutes.'

❹ The child goes away for a set amount of time. Put the kitchen timer on for the correct amount of time. Put the timer out of the child's reach.

❺ When the child hears the timer ring, they return with the work they have done.

❻ If they have followed the pattern of **listening** to the instructions, **repeating** them exactly, staying on task for the two or three or four minutes or whatever, and then have **returned** to you when the timer rings with the sequence **complete**, then they get a smiley face on their chart, and a big smile from you!

You are not giving the smiley face for the work they have done. It may or may not be good work. They get the smiley face for following the routine.

(Instructions to go on the back of the Careful Listening Chart)

Name ....

	Session One	Session Two	Session Three	Session Four
Monday				
Tuesday				
Wednesday				
Thursday				
Friday				

My careful listening chart

Case Overview – affix to outside of file

Name of child .... Date of Birth ....

Schools attended, with dates: ....

....

Stage One	Stage One Action Plan	Reviews

Date:
 	
Notes:
	Date: 1.
	        2.
	        3.
	Copy enclosed: Tick
	    1.
	    2.
	    3.
		Date: 1.
		        2.
		        3.
		Removed from register or move to Stage Two?
		
		Date:

Stage Two
Date:
 	
Notes:
	IEPs
	Date: 1.
	        2.
	        3.
	Copy enclosed: Tick
	    1.
	    2.
	    3.
		Reviews
		Date: 1.
		        2.
		        3.
		Returned to Stage One or move to Stage Three?
		
		Date:

Stage Three
Date:
Referral to outside agency?   Y/N
To whom?
1.
2.
3.
Date referred:
Copy of referral forms enclosed?   Y/N
	IEPs
	Date: 1. 4.
	        2.
	        3.
	Copy enclosed: Tick
	    1.
	    2.
	    3.
	    4.
		Reviews
		Date: 1. 4.
		        2.
		        3.
		Move to Stage Two or Three?
		Date:
		Notes:

Stage Four
Date of decision to move to stage four:
 	
Reports included: Tick
1.   Class Teacher
2.   SENCO
3.   E.P.
4.   Support service
5.   Others
6.   Copy of this overview sheet
	IEPs
	Date: 1.
	        2.
	        3.
	        4.
	Copy enclosed: Tick
	    1.
	    2.
	    3.
	    4.
		Reviews
		Date: 1.
		        2.
		        3.
		        4.
		Date sent for decision:
		Result:

Stage Five
Date Statement of Special Educational Needs Issued:
 	
Copy enclosed?
 	
Continuation sheet used?   Y/N
	IEPs
	Date: 1. 5.
	        2.
	        3.
	        4.
	Copy enclosed: Tick
	    1.
	    2.
	    3.
	    4.
	    5.
		IEP Reviews
		Date: 1.
		        2.
		        3.
		        4.

Case Overview (*contd.*) – affix to outside of file

Name of child .... Date of Birth ....

Date statement issued: ....

Annual Review	Reports	Summary of Review	IEPs
Date: Those invited: 1. 2. 3. 4. 5. 6. 7. 8. 9.	Received from: Copy enclosed?　　　Y/N 1. 2. 3. 4. 5. 6. 7. 8. 9.	Copy enclosed?　　Yes/No Copies sent to: 1. 2. 3. 4. 5. 6. 7. 8. 9.	Date: Copy enclosed?　　　Y/N 1. 2. 3. 4. 5. 6. Review set for: Dates: Copy enclosed?　　　Y/N 1. 2. 3. 4. 5. 6.
Annual Review	Reports	Summary of Review	IEPs
Date: Those invited: 1. 2. 3. 4. 5. 6. 7. 8. 9.	Received from: Copy enclosed?　　　Y/N 1. 2. 3. 4. 5. 6. 7. 8. 9.	Copy enclosed?　　Y/N Copies sent to: 1. 2. 3. 4. 5. 6. 7. 8. 9.	Date: Copy enclosed?　　　Y/N 1. 2. 3. 4. 5. 6. Review set for: Dates: Copy enclosed?　　　Y/N 1. 2. 3. 4. 5. 6.
Annual Review	Reports	Summary of Review	IEPs
Date: Those invited: 1. 2. 3. 4. 5. 6. 7. 8. 9.	Received from: Copy enclosed?　　　Y/N 1. 2. 3. 4. 5. 6. 7. 8. 9.	Copy enclosed?　　Y/N Copies sent to: 1. 2. 3. 4. 5. 6. 7. 8. 9.	Date: Copy enclosed?　　　　Y/N 1.　　　　4. 2.　　　　5. 3.　　　　6. Review set for: Dates: Copy enclosed?　Y/N 1.　　　　4. 2.　　　　5. 3.　　　　6.

Appendix 2
Resources

Training – Jenny Mosley Inset Courses

The following courses are available from Jenny Mosley Consultancies:

Promoting Happier Lunchtimes
Turn Your School Round – an introduction
A whole School Approach to building self-esteem
    through Circle Time
Assessing the effectiveness of your self-esteem,
    anti-bullying and positive behaviour policies
Raising morale through team-building
Practical activities to maintain and develop the power
    of Circle Time
Equal Opportunities
Curriculum enrichment
Drama and creative arts
Play therapy: an introduction course
Writing effective IEPs through Circle Time

Training Support for your workplace

The Jenny Mosley Consultancies has highly qualified personnel trained in the various areas of the Circle Time Model available to visit your workplace to give courses and workshops to all your teaching and support staff.

We run both closure and in-school days. In the former staff are invited to participate in a day that focuses on aspects of the Circle Time Model including team-building and developing moral values through Golden Rules, Incentives and Sanctions and ideas for Happier Lunchtimes.

During in-school days the Circle Time method is demonstrated with whole classes of children observed by a range of staff. In addition to this Circle Time meetings are held for lunchtime supervisors and an Action Plan for the school is considered with key members of staff.

Training the Trainer Courses

Key people may be trained either to go back to their school or their LEA as certified trainers responsible for supporting all adults and children in their community through the Jenny Mosley model.

For information on all the above courses contact: Jenny Mosley Consultancies, 8 Westbourne Road, Trowbridge, Wiltshire, BA14 0AJ.

Jenny Mosley Training Manuals and Resources

Mosley, J. (1993) *Turn Your School Round*, LDA.
Mosley, J. (1997) *Quality Circle Time*, LDA.
Mosley, J. (1996) *Golden Rules Posters*, LDA.
Mosley, J. (1996) *Class Target Sheets*, LDA.
Mosley, J. (1996) *Reward Certificates*, LDA.
Mosley, J. (1996) *Responsibility Badges*, LDA.
Mosley, J. (1996) *Stickers*, LDA.
Mosley, J. *Guideline for Midday Supervisory Assistants in Primary Schools*, Wiltshire Education Advisory Services, Courtney Hall, Trowbridge, Wiltshire.
Mosley, J. (1996) *Photocopiable Materials for use with the Jenny Mosley Circle Time Model*, Positive Press.

Other Circle Time and Self-Esteem Resources

Bliss, T. and Robinson, G. (1995) *Developing Circle Time*, Lucky Duck Publications.
Bliss, T. and Tetley, J. (1995) *Circle Time*, Lucky Duck Publications.

Curry, M. and Bromfield, C. (1995) *Personal and Social Education for Primary Schools through Circle Time*, NASEN Enterprises Ltd.

Fitzpatrick, P., Clarke, K. and Higgins, P. (1994) *Self-Esteem*, The Chalkface Project.

O'Brian, T. (1998) *Promoting Positive Behaviour*, David Fulton.

'Playgrounds in the Primary School', *Teaching Today*, BSS, PO Box 7, London.

Further ideas for the classroom

Feest, G. (1992) *Listening Skills: Activities for Primary School Children and Their Teachers*, Southgate Publishers Ltd.

Kingston Friends Workshop Group (1985) *The Handbook of Kingston Friends Workshop Group, Ways and Means: An Approach to Problem Solving.*

The Guide Association publish several activity packs appropriate for use with primary aged children. Atlantic Street, Broadheath, Altringham, Cheshire, WA14 5EQ.

The Gamesters Handbooks 1 and 2, by Donna Brandes, Hutchinson, are now out of print but are full of good ideas if you can get your hands on one!